To Susan:

"Through the years on earth,
and as eternity goes by,
The life and love He's given us
are never going to die." –Don Francisco

And Pa:

A good name is more desirable than great riches;
to be esteemed is better than silver or gold.

(Proverbs 22:1)

Section 1

A PIECE OF BOSCO

Who I am, and how I know God called me to be a juggler

40 Years a Juggler

It was a normal September day in 1976. Though school was back in session, the days were still long, so there was time for 14 year-old sophomore Richard Hagerstrom to gather together some neighborhood friends for a quick game of Whiffle ball before it was time to do homework. It was a day that would normally have been long forgotten these four decades later, except for the three plastic baseballs from Hagerstrom's cellar that, upon returning home, he neglected to put back downstairs. Like a typical 14 year-old boy, he tossed them on the living room couch and promptly forgot them.

Later that evening, while watching M-A-S-H, Richard watched as Alan Alda briefly juggled three pieces of fruit. Suddenly he remembered those three balls on the other side of the living room. With all the arrogance of a high school guy, he decided that he could juggle too, and his life was changed forever. Within days, he could keep three balls going in a basic pattern, and within weeks he was showing off at school and in his neighborhood.

Hagerstrom did a handful of shows throughout high school, including winning his high school talent show his senior year. At college, the demand for performances grew rapidly. His dorm had a day care center on the first floor, and one day he was juggling for the kids. Accidentally, lighting up a set of fire torches for his finale, he accidently triggered the building's smoke alarm, and all of his dorm-mates had to be evacuated!

"There was a bar in town," remembers Hagerstrom. "It was called Bauer's Back Room. Every April Fool's Day they had a talent contest. Hardly Vegas, but when I won in my junior year at University of Maine Farmington, I thought I had made the big time! Mostly I did shows at schools, granges, parties and around campus."

Fast forward to graduation: Richard found himself living in rural South Carolina. It was there, he says, that Jesus "swept me off of my feet into a relationship of grace that changed me forever." One change was what God had in store for his performances. His show quickly turned into a means to share God's Word, and demand for his program grew rapidly.

In 1986, ten years after that fateful day with the Whiffle balls, he moved backed to Maine and married Susan Legros, now his wife of 30 years. Together they continued using juggling, and the more newly-acquired skill of illusion, to share the Gospel in a wide range of settings. Hagerstrom remembers, "We enjoy doing shows in churches, but early on we knew that would not be our primary venue. God opened doors for us to do our ministry in jails, youth corrections, hospitals, colleges... a wide variety of settings. We learned a lot in those early years, and it was exciting to work hand in hand literally as husband and wife."

Richard and Sue have three daughters, all of whom have come through the family ministry. Jona-Lynn, now of Austin, Texas, incorporated juggling into a dance competition piece in high school, and it won her a gold medal. Naomi, now residing in New York, once entered a local talent show and won the $100 first prize as she demonstrated her skills with fire torches, machetes, fireballs and sickles. Their youngest, Rose, is 14, and can go into a full split while juggling three machetes.

The Hagerstroms, known as the Supreme Court Jesters, have performed in 18 states and five foreign countries, including missions trips to Mexico, Dominican Republic, Ecuador and Paraguay. "These trips have allowed us to share our program in a wide variety of unique settings: a women's prison high in the Andes, a city dump where families actually lived and raised their families, the holding pen for a slaughterhouse that doubled as the meeting place for a local AWANA club, even at the opening of Operation Christmas Child boxes.

We did a trip one time to the Crow reservation in Montana. We were part of a conference on missions work on reservations throughout the US. We were there to do children's ministry, but then, on the second morning, the leader of the conference told me he would be leaving early. He was on his way back to the Navajo reservation in Arizona for his grandson's birthday. He wanted me to close out the conference!

Rich continues: "At first, I was stunned. What experience did I have with evangelizing on reservations? Then I figured, 'Why not me?' I'd seen every episode of Dr. Quinn, Medicine Woman ever made. Seriously, though, it stretched our whole family quite a bit, but we saw the Lord work on that trip. He is so faithful."

This marks the 40th year since Richard Hagerstrom picked up those old Whiffle balls and began juggling. The Lord continues to use the Supreme Court Jesters to share the gospel in a range of settings. "Another 40 years will put us at 2056. I'll be 94. Then I might start to think about retiring from juggling, but I don't want to rush into it!"

To book the Supreme Court Jesters, call Richard Hagerstrom at (207) 647-3693 or e-mail to rhjugglesh@yahoo.com.

A Piece of Bosco

I think it was 1991 or 92. I was working late in my elementary resource classroom when a lady walked in. She introduced herself as a new member of the custodial staff at the middle school in town. She said she had heard I was a juggler, and she was, too. We talked shop for 20 minutes or so, and before she left, she gave me four back issues of Jugglers' World magazine from 1988.

Once I was home, I poured over the magazines, only to find an article entitled "A Patron Saint for Jugglers". It seems Father John Bosco, an Italian priest, was a juggler, magician and acrobat. He used his circus skills, in part, to attract attention from the street urchins at the market place, and then invited those who were orphaned to live in the orphanage he had started outside of town. Since I'm not a Catholic, I don't believe in patron saints, per se, but, since reading his biography and little bit of his own writings, he seems to have been a true believer in Jesus.

I never met that woman juggler before or since, but when we did meet, she happened to have magazines she was willing to give me. The magazines could have been any editions, but they happened to be from 1988, which is when JW happened to decide to run an article about Father Bosco.

But that's just the beginning of the story.

Almost twenty years later, my father died. It was January, 2000. All five of his sons and our families were with him for several days in a respite home as he was dying. This experience led me to reflect on my own life, and if I wanted to continue living the way I was living. It was not a crisis of faith; I knew Jesus was real and He was part of my life. But I wondered if my juggling was really a calling on my life, or just my way of 'Christianizing' what I wanted to spend my life pursuing.

That March, we were back in Vermont emptying my dad's house. When my brother, David, and I were cleaning out one room, he said, "What should we do with the piece of bone in that drawer?" I had no idea what he meant. He explained, "There's a little piece of bone in a plastic case. It's been around the house for years. I think it's a relic."

Sure enough, there was a small, plastic pendant with a relic inside. The case bore the name "Johannes Bosco". Neither one of us knew whose it was, so I found my oldest brother, John, and asked him about it. My first question was, "It says 'Johannes'. Is this John Bosco?" He confirmed that it was the same guy. Then my brother explained why we had a piece of Bosco.

He had gone to Catholic school, and one of his elementary teachers was a nun who also taught our mother. Because of this connection with the family, she wanted to give this sacred relic to my brother, John. It had been in our house ever since. My brother was happy to let me have the pendant to keep.

Understand, being Protestant, I do not view relics in the same way Catholic believers do. I don't think they have special, spiritual powers. It is just a bone fragment. But, when I consider that chain of events: A teacher just happens to have both my mother and brother as students. Of all those considered saints in the Catholic Church, she gives my brother a piece of John Bosco. We kept this object around the house for 40 years. A random meeting with a stranger led me to learn that Bosco was the patron saint of jugglers. I learned about the relic at a time in my life when I was wondering if juggling was really a serious way to minister to others. These events all put together gives me reassurance that I really do have a call from God to do what I continue to do to this day: serve God and others through juggling and magic.

A Little About My Church Background

I was raised Catholic by a very devout Catholic mother and a relatively nonreligious father. He always said he was raised Lutheran even though he went to a Methodist church. This was because his home town had no Lutheran church when he was a boy. When I was 14, my mother died, and it seemed to become more important to my dad that I continue going to church. Perhaps he was more religious than I thought. By my senior year in high school, when it was just him and me at home, we often went to the 8:00 PM Mass on Sundays, always commenting that it was a nice way to end the weekend and prepare for the following week of school and work. I love the quiet majesty of Catholic churches; the mood of reverence; the art work and architecture.

In college, I began to explore other churches. I finally settled into a Presbyterian church in a small town near where I attended school. I found it 'cool' that there was a family in the church who, although unrelated, shared my rare last name: Hagerstrom. Not exactly Smith or Jones.

That coincidence alone wasn't enough to keep me going there, though. I enjoyed the small size of the congregation, and the beautiful bike ride to church on Sunday mornings, especially in the fall. I appreciated how the congregation welcomed me right from the start.

After college, I got a teaching job in rural South Carolina. One day, at the laundromat, I saw a sign advertising a folk singer who would be performing at a local Methodist church.

This appealed to me, so I made a mental note of the date, and attended. This became my home church for three years. I loved the southern tradition of the Methodist church; the long history it had in the community; and I became good friends with the pastor's son. We started a ministry of juggling and illusions together. We are both still in full time Christian service today.

I moved back to New England when Sue and I married in 1986. We began attending an Assembly of God church. Quite different from anything I've experienced in the past. The pastor was very good about utilizing our juggling immediately, and our ministry grew rapidly. I loved the energy, the youth, the vision of this church.

When we moved to Bridgton, Maine and started a family, we joined the Bridgton Alliance Church, which is our home church today. More than any other, we feel like part of a family here. We love the part we play in this local body of believers, and we know that the other members of this body will be there for us when we need them.

So, it is this history that serves as a foundation of how I think about churches, denominations, and the universal body of Christ. These moves from church to church all had to do with relocation, not rebellion or hurt feelings. And in making these moves, I've learned a lot and feel we can minister for a lot of diverse groups without being uncomfortable or making others uncomfortable either.

Seven

Almost inevitably, when people learn I'm a juggler, the first question is, "How many balls can you juggle?" Every time I hear it, I cringe at this question for several reasons. First of all, the question shows a lack of appreciation of the real art of juggling. It is said that a juggler is only as good as his three ball routine. Numbers juggling is not the be all and end all of a good performance; In fact it's not even all that important to the quality of a show. Also, once given an answer, the questioner almost always follows up with, "Why can't you do... whatever the next number is?"

Furthermore, for me it's a hard question to answer. I consistently perform five balls, but I have only performed six a handful of times. In fact, I went decades, literally, without performing six before I was ready to reintroduce it. Even now, I only do it on rare occasions. Do I tell them I juggle five or six? There was even a time I was actually working on seven balls.

It was probably the mid 1990's when I was really striving to master this number. I remember stretches where I worked on it daily, and stretches when I let it rest for a period of time, but I never got it to the place where it was performable. At best, I could toss all seven balls and catch them all as well. More often, one or more of the balls succumbed to gravity and hit the floor with a thud.

I remember one day, though, when Sue, our oldest two girls and I were visiting my father at his Essex Junction, Vermont home, and, as I often did, I got up early in the morning and, after my first cup of coffee, went into his driveway and practiced my juggling. When I felt adequately warmed up, I took out my seven bean bag style juggling balls, and gave it a try. For the first and only time, I did eleven tosses with the seven balls, and caught them all; No drops whatsoever. I was thrilled.

Then I looked up at the kitchen window. My father had pushed the curtain aside and was watching. His applause was silenced by the closed window, but he was clapping and smiling broadly. I smiled back and held up seven fingers. His eyes got big and he mouthed the word 'Seven!?' I nodded.

But this silent exchange wasn't enough glory-basking for an accomplishment like this. I went inside, and over another cup of coffee, he and I relived the seven ball cascade I had accomplished with no less vigor and detail than if I had hit a game winning home run in the bottom of the ninth inning of the World Series.

After a few minutes of celebrating, I went back outside and finished my practice. However, I will never forget those few seconds where I nailed the hardest trick I've ever tried, unaware that an appreciative audience of one was looking on.

I always knew my dad was proud of me, not because I was always a great son, but because that's the type of man he was. But that morning it was something more intimate than fatherly pride. We had shared a moment that no one else in the world was privy to.

I never juggled seven so well again, and I haven't even tried it for many years. I probably never will try it again. It's certainly not essential to my performance, and it would be very time consuming to even approach mastery. It doesn't matter. My seven ball juggling was meant for that one moment in time and for my father and nobody else to share in.

I'll treasure that forever.

My Hero is a Woman I Never Met

(By our oldest daughter, Jona-Lynn)

You know how we elevate historical figures to such high levels and we have never met them? It is like we can just assume from the stories about them that they were amazing people. Basically we make heroes out of people we've never met. Well this is how I feel about my Grandma Joan Hagerstrom (She is where the first part of my name comes from). She is a woman I have never met but if I can be half the woman she was I will be more than pleased with myself.

My grandmother died when my dad was 14 so I never had a chance to meet her, however I do know all 5 of the boys she raised (my dad and his 4 older brothers) and for a hot second I knew the man she was married to (my Grandpa Roy). Just from knowing them I know she must have been an amazing woman. Grandpa was so in love with her, Joan was literally the love of his life. When he was in the hospice house (during the last few days of his life) he would wake up and tell everyone that he needed a haircut or a shave. He wanted these things because he knew he was going to see her soon and he wanted to look good for her. All my uncles and my dad are sweet men with very big hearts. That alone speaks volumes about who she was. It also tells me that she was a woman who could hold her own because she lived in a house with 6 men.

I want to be a woman who is very loving but is also strong.

The stories of my grandmother are what make me want to be like her. Grandpa would tell stories about growing up in New Jersey and how as a young man he worked for a gas station. He remembered this one family (the Walls) who had two little girls that would come to the gas station regularly.

One of the little girls, Joan, would always make kissy faces at him and she and her sister would giggle to each other in the back seat when he would pump their gas. Grandpa never thought anything of it because they were little girls and he was a teen. That's when WWII happened and my grandfather, like so many young men of the time, left for the war.

When he came back from the war he noticed that a very beautiful woman would walk by his house every day. He soon found out that that woman was Joan Wall. She would time her trips to the market around the time she knew he would be out in the garden (my grandfather was all about composting, that is one of the biggest memories I have of him). She did this for a few months and the only response she got was him stopping to talk to her every once in a while. One day she stopped at his fence, as she walked to the market, looked in him the eye and said "You know Roy I am 18 now!" and walked away.

I want to be a woman who knows what she wants and is stubborn enough to get it

Apparently on their first date (which soon followed that interaction) Grandma was so beautiful that Grandpa was distracted and drove over the highway median… I've always thought that actually meant that they were making out while he was driving.

My grandmother was a devoutly Catholic woman. She raised all 5 of her sons in the church and even sent the older ones to Catholic school. My dad was an altar boy as I'm sure was some of his older brothers.

I want to be a woman who raises her household in faith.

My dad (her youngest son) was born in 1961 so Joan lived in a very different world than we do. Everything was different including civil rights. For whatever reason, my grandmother ONLY used Black doctors. I don't really know why she liked Black doctors a lot more than White doctors I just know that this is something that was important to her. So much so that one of my uncles was born in the basement of the hospital because Black doctors were not allowed to perform deliveries where the White doctors did.

I want to be a woman who has convictions and sticks to them no matter circumstances.

To be honest, for most of my life I saw her as this perfect and magical woman not unlike Snow White or Clara from "The Nutcracker". Maybe she was (I certainly hope so). Regardless, I know that she was a strong woman, wife and mother. That alone is reason enough to look up to her and want to model myself after her.

There are some things about my grandmother that I'm not sure are true or just legends. I guess when one of her sons would spill something (which I'm sure happened a lot) she would say "Little girls NEVER spill." I have also heard that the Christmas when she and my grandpa were engaged she felt like he was dragging his feet and she said something to the effect of "do you even want to marry me?" I've also heard that her favorite color was green.

Donovan
(From 4/18/2012)

Last weekend Donovan was elected into the Rock and Roll Hall of Fame. This 60's British folk singer-turned psychedelic guru first hit the charts in 1965 with "Catch the Wind". His last top 40 hits were from his 1969 album "Barabajagal".

I remember my brother, David, bringing home an album entitled "The Pye History of British Pop Music: Donovan". It wasn't long before I was listening to it more than my brother. He left it in my care when he went to college, and shortly afterwards I had bought "The Pye History of British Pop Music: Donovan Volume 2". These two collections of his early folk work were always on my turntable. I would come home from high school, often to an empty house – I was the last to move out, my mom had died when I was a Freshman, and my dad would still be at work – and I would turn on the records, relax in the empty house and soak in the crystal vocals, the simple acoustic guitar work, and meditate on the lyrics. I felt like Donovan could read my mind as I listened to "Catch the Wind" and considered my own unrequited crushes. I weighed the merits on non-violence as I listened to "Universal Soldier". I dreamed of leaving home and juggling on the streets of Boston as I listened to "Rambling Boy". He was, in a real sense, a friend.

After two or three folk albums, his musical style switched dramatically, and he released "Sunshine Superman". I was not quick to embrace his new, more complex music with seemingly simpler lyrics. As I got older, though, I realized he was taking a lot of risks creatively as he became the first musician to dabble in jazz-fusion and world music. His song "Jennifer Juniper" mixed folk and classical sounds, "Hurdy Gurdy Man" is musical brilliance, and "Atlantis" introduced me to my favorite word, "antediluvian".

Although Donovan was one of the first celebrities to get involved in Hare Krishna, he inadvertently contributed significantly to the Jesus Movement of the 1970's. He wrote and performed the sound track for the movie "Brother Sun, Sister Moon". This movie, based on the life of Saint Francis of Assisi, had a huge following among the Jesus People, and is still relevant today. I remember my college roommate and campus Jesus freak singing the title song periodically.

Part of growing up is realizing that your heroes are not perfect, but can still be admired in their imperfection. Donovan is, to this day, a follower of Hare Krishna. Clearly, this means there are huge differences in our theological views.

Furthermore, some of his pre-conversion work was blatantly glorifying drug use, as even just the titles suggest: "The Trip", "Candy Man", "Mellow Yellow".

Nonetheless, I believe that, rather than an bad influence from my youth that I must avoid, his songs were one small, but not insignificant thing God used to form me into the person He would use years later. Every time I go on a ministry trip, somewhere in the back of my mind I'm hearing "Rambling Boy". Every time I read of wars and rumors of war, I hear "Universal Soldier". "To Try for the Sun" is the sound track always playing during the times I choose risk taking over security. Sometimes, when I hold my wife Sue's hand, I can almost hear these words from the song "Turquoise":

"Your smile beams like sunlight on a gull's wing
And the leaves dance and play after you.
Take my hand and hold it as you would a flower.
Take care with my heart, oh darling, it's made of glass."

Congratulations to Donovan for his well-deserved and long overdue election to the Hall of Fame. Thank you for the music, the innovation, and the company you were in an otherwise empty house in Vermont 35 years ago.

Amazing Grace
(A journal entry from 6/23/2011)

Like every other day in the past 49+ years, I sinned yesterday. This time, though, it was a bit louder and longer and angrier than in quite some time. The details, I suppose, are not important. Suffice it to say, I spent most of the afternoon angry and disappointed with myself, welcoming the condemnation of the enemy rather than bringing my broken, rebel heart to the cross.

One of the nice things about camp ministry, where we are now, is that we have services every evening. After an excellent sermon from my precious friend, Pastor Fred Shapiro, I knew it was time to face Jesus. In my prayer time, I told Him I truly regretted my actions, and more so, the condition of my heart, but, I thought, I'll probably do the exact same thing tomorrow. The Holy Spirit interrupted me right then, and, as if whispering into my contrite spirit, 'said' "Yes, and my grace will still cover you tomorrow, too. Do you really think you have more sin in you than I have grace in me?"

All too often I think of myself first, even when it seems spiritual. "I need to grow", "I'm so sinful", "I should do better." In reality, that's still pride, although it's not arrogance. Arrogance is thinking I'm better than others. Pride is simply thinking of me instead of others, or, like yesterday, instead of thinking accurately about God.

I've prayed a lot today, at least for me, and I've read about grace in my devotional time, but I haven't really entered into the time of day I'm most prone to this particular type of temptation. In truth, I have no idea how I'll do when temptation is all in my face again.

But I do know that God will be there extending a grace that is far stronger and longer lasting than anything, good or bad, that I do today. Now that's amazing.

How a Kid I Met at a Show and Didn't Really Like Changed my Life

We were doing a show recently, and afterwards I met a teenage boy who told me he juggled 'a little.'

Right... a little.

Actually, he was outstanding, and he even could flash 8 balls. At my best, in the 1990's, I flashed 7.

He accomplished things in two years of juggling that I never have done in 35 years. Sure, he was polite, respectful, and articulate. But nice as he was, I decided right away I couldn't like him. After all, he was so much farther along than I was at his age.

I know that's shallow.

I'm kidding.

Kind of.

Yeah, I'm kidding.

I guess.

But, he taught me a trick called multiplexing that I'd seen performed but never fully understood. It's simple but looks complicated.

Not only that, but there's lots of variations of multi-plexing. This little technique has improved my juggling more than anything I've learned in the past several years. And, it's fun!

Maybe that kid's all right after all.

<u>Birthdays</u>
(Journal entry from 12/21/2011)

In six hours I'll be doing something I've done 50 times before; I'll celebrate a birthday. I'm told that the day I was born I weighed 12 pounds! Apparently, another new father was bragging in the waiting room about his son who was 10 pounds, and a hospital staff person told him, "This man's son is twelve pounds!" One of the times they brought the babies to their mothers in the nursery, we were all brought out in Christmas stockings. Unfortunately, I didn't fit, so they split the stocking down the seam and draped it over me. When my father came home for a meal, he told my older brothers, "He's so fat he's almost repulsive!"

I don't remember many specific birthdays as a child. Since it is three days before Christmas, a lot of my memories are a blur of the two events in one memory. I do remember one birthday party where I was given a kaleidoscope. I'm not sure who I got it from, but it was an amazing gift: all the changing colors and images were mesmerizing.

In third grade I had a big birthday party. My best friend from school, Tommy Tiller came, and he was most excited to see my pet turtle, Gilligan. I was equally excited to show off my shelled little buddy. I don't remember much else about the party, but I do know that Tom Tiller became the CEO of Polaris and retired before the age of 50.

I can't say I remember recent birthdays much better than the early ones. My 22nd birthday, however, is unforgettable. I was home from my first year teaching in South Carolina, and I had borrowed my brother's car to go visit friends at my old college. Desiring to get home on my birthday, I headed to Vermont from Maine in a snowstorm; I crashed my brother's car, totaling it. Skidding in the snow, I lost control approaching a bridge and swerved to the right. I crashed into the guard rail of the bridge and slid across to the other side. Had I swerved left first, I would have been hit straight on by a pulp truck carrying a load of logs heading in the other direction. I could have easily died. When I think of God's grace, this is often the first image that comes to my mind.

I was also driving on my 30th birthday. I was coming home from a late meeting in the school district where I worked, and flipped on the radio. I heard the song "Turning Thirty" by Randy Stonehill for the first time. Expecting our first child at that time, I loved a line that went "I've got a wife who really loves me, she makes my life complete, and a little baby daughter, she plays games around my feet..."

Tomorrow I'm turning 50. That little baby daughter, who was yet unborn on my 30th birthday, is a sophomore in college, and about to go to Cambodia to work with churches and nongovernment agencies to fight human trafficking. They'll even minister to young girls in brothels there.

Two more 'little baby daughters' have followed her into the world. The car crash that could have taken my life was over half my life ago. Little pet turtles like the one that fascinated the future Fortune 500 CEO are no longer legal to sell in the state of Maine. The song "Turning Thirty" is still a favorite of mine, but thirty sounds so young now. Our lives are truly a mist that lifts quickly. "Teach us to count how few days we have, that we may gain wisdom of heart." Ps. 90:12.

Adam and Eve and Richard and Susan

I believe that when you look at the evidence objectively, not being swayed by the fire-and-brimstone fundamentalists on the one side, or the late night satirical comics on the other, there is a lot of scientific support for Creationism / Intelligent Design and not nearly as much the is assumed to be for evolutionary theory. That being said, I do wonder what theological conclusions can clearly be drawn from the first three chapters of Genesis, and which ones are conjecture. At one end of the spectrum, there are the theological ideas that are repeated again and again in Scripture, and believers have held for centuries: For example, ever since Adam and Eve rebelled, that fallen nature- original sin- has been part of the human race is a doctrine reiterated by Jesus, Paul, and the Apostles' and Nicene Creeds.

On the other dubious extreme, I once read an article about a community of Christian nudists who believe that, since clothes came after the fall, and Christians are no longer 'under the curse' clothing was no longer needed or even a particularly good thing. There's a whole array of Genesis-based theology in between.

One portion of the creation story that has spawned a huge variety of doctrines is when it tells us that Eve was created to be Adam's helpmate. Before God made woman, apparently He paraded all the animals in front of Adam, but none were a fit mate for him. YA THINK!

Did an all knowing God really think Adam would settle for a rhinoceros or a pigeon instead of holding out for a beautiful naked woman? That aside, what does it mean when God called Eve Adam's helpmate? Was it an arrangement specifically for just the first couple? Was it a principle that would work for most couples, but not a biblical absolute? Or is it the model that all marriages are to be based upon?

It's important to note that the Bible is full of strong, independent women. Mary, Sarah, Esther, and Elizabeth, for example, all showed much more confidence in God than their husbands did. Deborah was a Judge of Israel, and an excellent one at that. Just the fact that there are two Bible books named for heroines makes the Old Testament radically feminist for its era.

So, we can conclude that 'helpmate' is not synonymous for doormat, sex kitten or maid. And it is with this in mind that I state that I am married to a wonderfully strong, faithful, hardworking helpmate. This weekend she repaired three very different types of props that were showing wear. And she did this with odds and ends of materials lying around the house.

Sue is not one to get in front of an audience, but I couldn't do my ministry without all she does behind the scenes. But, she's every bit as competent in her roles of adult educator, mother, mentor, and unpaid 'counselor' to countless less confident women, to name just a few of the hats she wears.

But she's more than the sum of her roles. She's my best friend, by confidante, and she is prettier now than when we first got married 26 years ago this month. Often, I look across the living room and see her snuggled in a blanket reading a book with her beautiful long hair flowing over her shoulders, and I can't believe how blessed I am.

I'm glad Adam didn't settle for a rhino or a pigeon!

Section 2

STORIES FROM THE ROAD

You can't juggle for 40 years and not have stories to tell

Car Keys and Pharisees

On December 30th, I had a show at the York County Jail, in Alfred, Maine. A large group of inmates came to the show, and there was a presence of peace that was noticed not only by the chaplain, but some of the guards working there as well. It was truly a special day.

But I did something that day, that I almost never do... I locked my keys in the car! While waiting for AAA to arrive to unlock the van, I was standing with an inmate who was waiting for a ride to his work release site. After finally hanging up with AAA, I shared my woes with him. Suddenly, I was getting a rather in depth lesson on all the ways someone could get into a locked car! He admitted to owning six 'slim jims', the thin metal devices designed to open locked cars. He told me about other household items that could unlock a car, and how to prevent setting off side air bags. He even told me that Jaguars were the hardest cars to break into, but he could do it in under five minutes.

Then I told him I was there for a chapel service. Suddenly, he told me he himself had NEVER broken into a car, and these were just things he knew from 'working on cars.' It was all very amusing.

Isn't it funny how people think they need to present their best sides when they learn someone is a Christian... even if their best sides aren't truly them at all? How different this is from how Jesus dealt with people. Yes, he pointed out their sins, as was the case with the woman at the well.

But the fact is, the people who Jesus most strongly rebuked weren't the flagrant sinners, but the religious elite who refused to humbly own their sins and shortcomings. I wonder what He would have said to my new friend that day in the York County Jail.

That's My Dad

A few summers ago, we were juggling at a Vacation Bible School picnic in northern Maine. Our youngest daughter, Rose, was probably five or six years old. It was as if it were the first time she realized that other people thought juggling was a pretty special thing. Until then, it was something she assumed all fathers did out in the backyard just like her father does, but suddenly she noticed how many kids and adults were laughing, applauding and excited about flaming torches, machetes and the like flying through the air. Above all the noise of a church picnic, I began to hear her voice, "That's my dad! That's my dad!" She wanted everyone there to know that she was related to the guy who was drawing so much attention.

Tonight as I watch yet another Maine storm drop tremendous amounts of snow into our yard, I marvel at the beauty and magnitude of God's handiwork. I want to shout to the world, "That's my Dad. That's my Dad! Isn't He cool! Look what He can do! You can *watch* what He's able to do, but I KNOW Him. It's my Dad doing that!" I'm a child of the Creator of all. Now that's grace.

He's an American Bird

A couple of summers ago, we had a show on a Sunday morning just over the Canadian border, in Woodstock, New Brunswick. For some reason, only my daughter Naomi and I went, which is not all that uncommon. We crossed into Canada without a problem, did a church service at a Wesleyan church, and headed back to Maine. At the border, coming back into the USA, the border guard was appalled to see that we had our dove with us. "You can't bring a bird across the border!"

"But," I replied, "He's an American bird. We just brought him in to do a magic show. He's only been in Canada for about three hours!"

We were told we needed to go back to Canada until Tuesday, when the border vet would be in his office.

"Border vet?"

Obviously, we couldn't stay in Canada for two extra days, so the guard told us to park our van and come inside. "But the bird stays in the van!"

We were at a small town border crossing on a Sunday morning, so as we entered the building, we were the talk of the officers. "He has a bird! They're the ones with the bird!" they whispered. Instead of fear or shame, Naomi and I came down with a severe case of the giggles. Border guards, it seems, don't like the giggles.

After being yelled at a little by a guard who was built a bit like Fred Flintstone, we decided we would bring our dove back to Canada and see if anyone at the church would take care of him until Tuesday. We drove back to the church, but it was locked and no one was around. We left our dove, Salt, on the porch of the church with a note, reminiscent of Little Orphan Annie.

We returned to the border and told the guards that we left the bird with some friends, and we passed into the states without a problem. But we still needed to get Salt back from our neighbors to the north.

So, after leaving our bird in Canada on the front porch of a church, Naomi and I returned without incident to our summer camp in Mapleton, Maine. We were given two pieces of information that we thought would be helpful: 1) the border vet would be in again on Tuesday, and 2) We now had his home veterinary office phone number in Houlton, Maine.

On Monday morning, I called his home office, hoping at least to get some direction in how to proceed, as well as an estimate of how much it would cost to get our bird back. However, the receptionist at the vet's office said she neither she nor the doctor could discuss international pet issues from the Maine office. I would have to call him at the border the next day. The one thing I was able to do was to call the church and see if Salt had been found.

Sure enough, the neighbor's girl saw him on the church's steps and brought him in for the night, then brought him to the church when the offices opened in the morning. I explained that they would need to get some bird seed for him, as this was going to take longer than we expected.

On Tuesday I called the vet at his border office. He was expecting my call. He said that our best bet was to have Salt declared 'poultry', which he said was defined as a 'necked bird'. If he was a pet bird, it would cost a lot more, take a lot longer, and may even require the Feds from Boston to come up before we could get him back! The doctor said he would check with his Canadian counterpart to see what could be done for us.

Later that day, I got the return call from the border. The vet told me that the Canadians were very embarrassed by the whole situation, since Salt never should have entered their country to begin with. They wanted to make the whole thing 'go away.' So, as far as Canada was concerned, Salt never entered their country to begin with! The vet would not be at the border again until Thursday, but I could come up then and get my dove back. In a word, my bird was being deported! I got him back later that week, and he worked for us for another two years. But he never left the country again.

Bridgton Health Care

This morning I did a show at the local nursing home in Bridgton, Maine. Being the day before Easter, I felt there were better things I could be using my time for, especially since I have performed there as recently as two months. But, of course, I went.

I used the Easter season to talk about waiting for God's best timing. I shared how the disciples waited three days before the resurrection, Mary and Martha waited four days for Lazarus to be brought back to life, the world waited for centuries for the prophecies of Christ to be fulfilled, etc.

After the show, a resident in the front row called me over and asked if I recognized her. I confessed I did not. She said she was Bertha, a lady who, in better health, was a regular at our home church. Then she said, "The Lord's having me wait for Him, you know." I knew immediately what she meant. She wanted to go to heaven.

I responded, "But think of what a celebration it will be when that day finally arrives." Suddenly she lit up like a child anticipating her birthday party.

"I probably shouldn't say it," she replied, "But I can't wait until I go." I reminded her that even the Apostle Paul longed for the day he'd go home to be with Jesus. I knew, then, why I had gone there today.

Honestly, I don't think much about heaven, yet. When I do, I'm glad that Jesus has made a way for me to go, but I can't say I'm anxious to go...it just beats the alternative. No doubt I feel this way because I still have three young daughters (yes, teenagers are still *young* daughters), a beautiful wife, a good job and an active ministry. But my conversation with Bertha today reminded me that heaven is not just 'better than the alternative', it is our hope, and, in truth, our home. We are, after all, only visiting this planet. Thank you, Bertha, for reminding me of what Easter is all about.

Epilogue:

In less than two weeks, we received the news that Bertha's prayers had been answered, and she was in Heaven. Her wait is over.

The Hymns are Hers

20 years ago we did a show that I remember vaguely, at best. We met a local singer named Thelma Kilbreth. To the best of my knowledge, we never met again, but she gave us a copy of a tape of hymns she had recorded. We kept it, listening to it occasionally.

Then, 15 years ago, we were invited to share our show at a local Baptist church, with one stipulation: Any music we used had to be hymns. I could have tried to get them to change their minds, accepted the show but used our regular music against their wishes, or turned down the show and write them off as intolerant and narrow-minded. Or... try to make it work. We decided to try to make it work. We used two songs off of Thelma's tape. I created a balance board routine to "Standing on the Promises of God" and a hat juggling routine to "Crown Him with Many Crowns". I still use both of these routines from time to time today.

Last night we had a show at the Auburn, Maine Advent Christian Church. I had no intention of using these routines there, because it was primarily an outreach to unchurched, inner city families. Most of the audience wouldn't know the old hymns or even appreciate them musically. But I kept thinking that we should do "Standing on the Promises". It made no sense, but I went with it. What could it hurt?

After the show a couple came up to us and introduced themselves. They were Pastor and Thelma Kilbreth. We told them the story of how we came to use her music in our show, and joked about owing her years of royalties. They told us they could get us the same music on CD, which will be a real blessing. Tapes are old school, even for me, and when it eventually breaks I wouldn't have had any way to replace it. Now I do. Furthermore, she was blessed to learn that her music has been used all over New England and beyond for the last 15 years.

Thank you, God, for your divine appointments that we simply call coincidence.

John 3:16

I remember a show early in our ministry at a nursing home in Vermont. As we were setting up our props prior to the show, the staff began bringing in the residents a few at a time in their wheelchairs. One lady, clearly a dementia patient, was very agitated, and began yelling random phrases and words that were irrelevant to the setting. Professionals call this behavior perseveration.

Sue and I realized that we would not be heard at all during the show if this behavior continued, and it was clear the resident wouldn't be stopping any time soon. So we stepped outside and prayed. We prayed for the lady, for the other residents who'd be at the show, and the performance itself. We prayed for our own attitudes. Then we went back inside.

Remarkably, the lady was silent throughout the entire show! We knew immediately that this was answered prayer. But God was not done. As soon as the show was over, the lady began perseverating again, only now it was not meaningless gibberish. Instead, the resident began yelling, over and over, "For God so loved the world that He gave His only Son, that whoever believes in Him shall not perish, but have eternal life."

What happened in the lady's heart that day? I don't know. But God is able to reach into the hearts of anyone who still has breath, regardless of disability, presence of mind, age or any other factor. How do I know? "For God so loved the world…

Most Embarrassing Moments

Here are some of my most embarrassing moments as a juggler:

1) At family day for a group home for disabled adults in northern Maine, I was performing one of my regular routines. In this three ball routine, I keep juggling the three balls as I gradually lay flat on my back, then come back up to a standing position. At this particular show, as I slowly stood back up, I split my pants!

2) Years later, at a family day event for a nursing home in southern Maine, we were again performing outdoors. This time it was on a very hot June day. After the show, the son of one of the residents came up to me and said, "Your faith is inspiring." Unfortunately, I heard, "Your face is perspiring," so I responded, "That happens a lot, especially in the summer!"

3) At a campground in the White Mountain region of New Hampshire, I was doing an audience participation routine with a 10 year old girl. In the routine, I dress my volunteer up in the armor of God (from Eph. 6) made from balloons. The young girl got giggling harder and harder as the routine progressed. Finally, near the climax of the show, she couldn't control herself any more, and she wet her pants in front of the whole audience!

4) At an elementary school in Kentucky, some bats that lived back stage decided to use show time as their time to come out and fly around the auditorium. The audience was in a panic! Finally, the principal decided there was no settling the kids back down, and she cut the assembly short. On the way out of the show, one little boy said to me in a thick Kentucky accent, "I really liked that trick when you made those bats fly around the room!"

5) Before starting a show in Quito, Ecuador, our translator asked if we were ready to go. I gave him the "OK" sign, thumb and index finger touching, the other three fingers pointing up. We wondered why there was a collective gasp from the audience until later when our translator told us the "OK" sign was actually a profanity in Ecuador!

6) Returning home from a trip to Maryland, I decided that I didn't want to trust the airlines with my bag of props, so they became my carry on... until the x-ray machine at the Washington, DC airport picked up on the three machetes inside. It was scary for a while, but eventually they let me check the bag instead of carry it on.

Why Would we Bring Rose (Age 11) to Paraguay

Occasionally people have asked us if our kids go with us on short term mission trips. They always have. In fact, Naomi's toilet training was done partially on a bus in Mexico. Rose learned to go up and down stairs at the mission house in Ecuador. Now that our two oldest girls are in college, they are not part of this current trip to Paraguay, but Rose is. Here are some of the benefits we see in having brought her:

> She has become fast friends with Megan, an 11 year daughter of one of our host missionaries.

> In our recent trip to Ciudad Del Este, she and Megan played with daughters of two different Chilean missionary families. At one point the girls were running pretty wildly through the apartment playing some version of keep away. Megan acted as translator.

> A Chilean missionary, Octavia, gave her own hand carved Chilean toy as a thank you for Rose's mission work. This is a truly priceless gift.

> Rose took it upon herself to share the Gospel story with a squatter woman after a show in a vacant lot / cattle pen.

> Rose has been interacting with kids and teens that don't speak the same language and had been communicating and interacting with them joyfully.

> We stayed in the home of Baptist missionaries in Ciudad Del Este. They have an 18 year old daughter, Jade, still living at home. The three girls hit it off despite the age difference. This missionary family fled Venezuela when Hugo Chavez wanted all Venezuelan youth to 'belong' to his military. Then, on the 4th of July, Jade had the privilege of singing the American and Paraguayan national anthems at the American embassy here in Asuncion. Rose actually got to hang out with a teenager who experienced all of that.

> She not only visited but ministered in a church where the congregation included people from Lebanon, China, Pakistan , Chile, India, and of course, Paraguay.

> She has seen Iguazu Falls, one of the new 7 natural wonders of the world.

> She has seen people living in tents made of garbage bags and seen that they are no less human than she is.

> She's seen a monkey and dozens of coatis in the Brazilian jungle.

She is having a wonderful, meaningful experience here, and we would never deny her this. She is seeing a world beyond her usual world and seeing God work here as surely as he works at home.

Payment in Full

Over the years, I have been paid for performances in a variety of unique ways. In college, I did a show at a local elementary school, where I was reimbursed with a dozen hand blown glass Christmas tree ornaments the art teacher had made. It was just within the last year or two that the last of these fragile ornaments broke.

Another time in college, I did a show for a local grange and was paid with a pound of homemade fudge and a flashlight. Homemade fudge was certainly a unique treat in the dorm, and the flashlight came in handy, too. I was often up later than my roommate, and this allowed me to come in at night without waking him by turning on the big light.

After marrying Sue, we did a show for a family's party. They paid us with an assortment of moose meat. Apparently the father had hit and killed a moose with his truck, and the state of Maine allows the driver to keep meat in such cases.

On the Crow reservation, we were reimbursed with handmade, authentic jewelry, a leather wallet and dream catchers. A teen center once sent us home with a case of Sobe flavored waters.

Another family made new shirts for our family to wear when performing in payment for juggling at a party. Years ago, when I juggled with an elementary aged boy, he was 'paid' with a Tonka truck after performing at a Salvation Army drug rehab house.

Then, this week, Rose and I did a show at a local school's Bible club. They paid us generously, but they also donated two Bibles in our names through the Gideon's' ministry. This was a huge blessing to us. The Gideon's is a ministry that distributes Bibles worldwide. Where will our two Bibles end up? Perhaps in hotels, hospitals or jails. Perhaps in the hands of college students. Perhaps on the foreign mission field. We will probably never know, but what a great way to be reimbursed for a show.

I encourage more people to give alternative gifts-Bibles, child sponsorships, animals for third world families - when possible. Look into ministries such as the Gideon's, Gospel for Asia, Compassion International, the Salvation Army, Teen Challenge and many others you can find on line or through your own church or denomination.

Most Unique Settings

These are some of the most unique settings we've performed in.

1) The city dump in Quito, Ecuador. People live there in order to find clothing, food, and shelter. Sometimes they find things they can sell in the street for a little money. We went twice with teenagers from Alliance Academy who visit each week to provide food, hygiene, and educational opportunities. One of our visits was Naomi's 12th birthday.

2) The women's prison, also in Quito. Women from five continents were there, mostly for running drugs. They serve seven year sentences often with their children having to live there with them. Many of the women have to prostitute themselves to pay their 'rent' on their cells. One of our shows was in the courtyard, where teenaged guards looked down on us from the watchtowers, armed with machine guns. I did not take my machetes out of my bag.

3) A cow pasture in Santo Domingo, Dominican Republic. Some church members strung up some lights and made a makeshift stage. Cattle roamed around as the Dominican musicians played, I juggled, and a young seminarian preached. Watch where you step!

4) Weddings. We have been part of the 'entertainment' at three wedding receptions.

5) My brother's driveway. Many years ago, when I was just out of college, I was staying with my oldest brother and his family. I was practicing there when his daughter came walking home from school with a group of friends. Spontaneously, I turned my practice session into a show for the kids.

6) My father's kitchen. My father had neighbors whose little girl often came over to visit him. One time, Sue and I were there when the little girl and a friend were over. We talked about our show, and I told them, "Get some of your friends from the neighborhood, and I'll do a show here in 20 minutes." They did, and I did.

7) A ministers' conference on the Crow Indian Reservation in Montana. What was unique here is that I am 100% Caucasian, but I was asked to be the closing speaker at a conference on the reservation for Indian pastors on the theme of how to minister to Native peoples.

8) A local grocery store. A store in Naples, Maine has a Christmas open house every year. Our church's music ministry, puppet team, and our family have performed there several years in a row.

9) Bars. Before we had children, it was common for Sue and me to go to bars that were having open mic nights. We'd get on the program and do our Gospel presentation when our turn came up. Sometimes we were heckled, often we were applauded, once we were threatened, but we ALWAYS had people come up to us after our programs to share their problems, tell us of the faith of their mothers or grandmothers or wives, and even book us to come to their homes and perform at family parties!

10) A corn maze. Locally, there was a corn maze that was a fund raiser for a program for battered women. As people lined up to enter the maze, we juggled for them, right there by the side of the road.

LOL (My Team of Middle School Jugglers) Goes to Connecticut: May, 2013

Every school year, I bring my middle school juggling team, LOL, on an end of the school year four or five day out of state trip to perform, present the Gospel and serve each other. I just got home from this year's trip to Willimantic, CT. We did six shows in four days.

Willimantic is an old mill city where the mills have shut down. Consequently, there is a lot of poverty, homelessness and drugs. Although it is a city of 18,000 people, it feels much more like the inner city, especially the downtown area where we were staying. In fact, a 60 Minutes piece about Willimantic aired in 2009 started this way:

"This is a story about a small town in New England that has a problem you'd never expect. Heroin. It's a problem that has existed for decades. It's been so bad for so long that some people call the place 'Heroin Town.'" (See entire transcript here: http://www.cbsnews.com/2100-500164_162-557978.html)

This year's trip was special for me right from the start because my wife Sue was able to free up her schedule to be one of the chaperones. Since we were both going to be gone, we also freed up our sixth grade daughter, Rose. LOL is made up of 7th and 8th graders only, so Rose was not performing (she gets plenty of stage time with me throughout the year, so this was no big deal for her.) She did enjoy hanging with the team and getting to know some of the kids she'll be in LOL with next year.

I always organize our team into student led work groups. These groups do the loading, unloading, cleaning and cooking for the four days. There is also an adult chaperone assigned to each work group, but the goal is to make the adults do as little as possible: they're there to solve problems that arise and assure safety, especially in the kitchen. As always, the kids rose to the challenge and worked very hard.

I had a total of six chaperones: myself, Sue, my classroom aide Amanda, Angie who is the mom of a student, and two dads: Bob who is our school's maintenance guy, and Duane, a state trooper. Each one was vital to the team.

Our contact in Willimantic was Pastor Fred Shapiro of First Baptist Church. He is a longtime friend and co-laborer in ministry. We have worked together throughout New England since 1991. Fred is also a tremendous blues singer and pianist. His song "Jesus is Victor" is a staple in both my class's show and my own. It is the perfect high energy juggling tune.

We arrived at First Baptist at about 2:00, and moved into the church basement: boys in fellowship hall, girls in Sunday school room. Our first show was that evening, and upon returning to the church we had a class chapel service. I had prayed extensively about what to speak on, and I ended up doing a message about risk taking.

I had no idea what a perfect topic this would be throughout our stay there. The following days would challenge the students in many unexpected and growth producing ways. As a 7th grade girl has already posted on Facebook, "The Connecticut trip was life changing."

Sleeping peaceably in a strange place is often difficult, and this was certainly true of our first night in Willimantic. The fact that we were on tile floors (Sue was smart and bought an air mattress for the trip) and the kitchen work team inadvertently left the industrial sized kitchen fan on all night, thus sucking the heat out of the building, made sleeping all the harder. Nevertheless, the LOL team woke up eager to start their first full day in Connecticut.

Our first show of the day was in a local nursing home. To me the best part of this program was after we had finished the show. The students are taught to interact with the audience after a show, bring around the chicken and rabbit we use, pray for the people if they'd like, etc. When the rest of the team had packed up all the props and was out of the building, Rose was still inside with two other girls on the team ministering to one of the female residents. She was fitting right in with the class already.

Our afternoon show was at Nickerson's Family Campground. Owned by a Christian couple, the campground offers Sunday services and Christian entertainment (that would be us) but its clientele is by no means all believers in Jesus. We arrived early as the Nickerson's graciously let us use their campground showers while we were there. Our show was on an outdoor stage, and I was surprised by how many people were camping there on an April weekend. We probably had an audience of 50 or more. This was our only outdoor venue of the year, which created certain challenges for some kids. Stephanie walked on the high stilts on rough ground, Lucy and Kat juggled rings in the breeze, and our dancers danced on the lawn. They all rose to the occasion.

Since the school year is coming to a close, I use shows during this trip to highlight 8th graders as they will be graduating out soon. So at this performance Makayla did a juggling solo routine. She was great. She performed machetes and fire torches for the first time, in a routine that also included clubs and juggling three balls with a chicken on each shoulder. The whole idea of a solo was a risk for her as Makayla is a reserved young lady. Her progress has been amazing, though. She ended 7th grade only able to juggle silks. She has worked very hard this year.

Once we were showered and packed, I stopped by the camp office to thank the owners. That's when he told me something that is one of the highlights of the trip. He explained that there is a family who has been camping here for 15. They are not Christians and have never attended any of the services the campground provides, except once. Five years ago, they went to a service there and walked out half way through. After we did our show, they went to the camp office and asked the owner what time church was the next day because they wanted to attend. The kids are what changed their minds!

After returning to our base, having dinner, a trip to Dairy Queen and evening chapel, we settled in for sleep. The hard floor suddenly didn't seem so uncomfortable, and everyone was asleep quickly.

When the LOL juggling team woke up on Sunday morning, they had their work cut out for them. The fellowship hall and Sunday school rooms which had been the male and female dorms for the team had to be returned to their normal state for the soon-to-be-arriving worshippers. While one work team prepared breakfast, the other LOLers packed up and picked up and the building was ready for use with time left over.

Sunday was a day of surprises and opportunities to spotlight individual students. Noah was chosen to do his 8th grade juggling solo during the morning service, and he did a fine job, ending with a blazingly fast 3 machete cascade. But he was only one of several students who were in the spotlight in new ways.

An hour and a half before his service started, Pastor Fred called me and told me his worship leader had the flu. "Do you have anyone in your group who could lead singing?" Immediately I thought of Brandon. Only 14, he has already led worship in his own church and leads the middle school class each week at school. I handed him the phone, and he and Fred had things planned out a short time later. Together, they sang "Jesus is Victor", a song both LOL and the Supreme Court Jesters use in their shows, as well as a few other worship songs. With Fred on keyboard and Brandon on guitar, they sounded excellent.

Fred had also asked me to have a student ready to share a brief testimony. I made an unlikely choice when I asked Amanda F. (a student, not the aide). There are many other students who are more comfortable speaking in public, but I really felt she was the one. In the end, she spoke about how God helped her through the death of a friend. Amanda was confident, poised, had great eye contact, and spoke with clarity and passion. Later that day an older woman from the church told her how much her testimony blessed her as she had been through something similar.

After we did our 20 minute set, Pastor went on with the service. We were asked to provide six students to help with their children's church time downstairs. Unfortunately, I misunderstood and thought their leader would have a plan and my students would just assist. They thought my students would do more routines. When there's a room full of little kids with nothing to do, it is a potential disaster. However, led by Alex, the students adlibbed and later the teacher raved about how well they did. Alex especially demonstrated the ability to think on his feet, I was told.

We had our first significant free-time Sunday afternoon. We explored downtown Willimantic. Then some on the team went to the local mall while others stayed at the church and rested. The down-time was well timed, because our biggest moments were to come that night.

Sunday evening, our team went two different directions. Pastor Fred has a weekly Gospel radio show and asked if a couple of kids wanted to go with him to the studio. Brandon, who is interested in music production, was an obvious choice. I also selected Lucy, as she is an 8th grader, would present herself well on the air, and she has been in LOL for two consecutive years. One of our chaperones, Bob, who is also Brandon's father, went too.

The rest of the team did our regular program at Fred's church for a meal ministry they host five times per week. There is a large homeless and low income population in this city, and they actually get more people to their meals than at their Sunday morning services. Because we were performing while the others were on the radio, we didn't get to hear the whole show, but we are told that Lucy and Pastor Fred had a lengthy debate on the air regarding which is better: *American Idol* or *the Voice*. We did get to hear most of Brandon's air time as he and Fred discussed music production, and one of Brandon's compositions was played on the air! He came back that night very inspired.

Meanwhile, back at the church, we were playing to a packed house. The fellowship hall was crowded, and the line between the stage area and the drinks and salad dressing table was a bit blurred at times, but the kids have become confident and capable enough this year that they were able to adjust as the show was going. The most extreme example of this adaptability was when we were performing a mime set to music called "I Want to Know What Love Is". In this skit, set to the old Foreigner tune, Noah sits on a park bench with a heart shaped balloon. He offers it to girl after girl as they walk by, only to be rejected each time. At one point, Amanda accepts the offer of his heart only to have Erik confront them and pull Amanda away with him. At this point, Erik delivers a very convincing stage punch to Noah's face.

After the mock blow to the head, a man in the crowd who was clearly high yelled at Erik and went on the stage to assist Noah. Several seconds passed before the head of the food ministry realized what happened and escorted the man off of the stage. But here's the amazing part: Noah never broke character. Clearly he saw the man approaching. Clearly he knew the man was confused, even if he didn't recognize him as under the influence. Clearly we had prepared them with the knowledge that street people were potentially dangerous. But Noah continued to play his part and stay in character. Now that's a real pro.

After the program was finished, three of the clientele prayed with me to receive the grace and forgiveness of Jesus, which made it a perfect ending to a perfect, albeit lengthy, day.

We spent one more night on the church floor before we headed back to Maine on Monday morning, but the kids left a piece of their collective hearts in Connecticut.

Operation Silent Night

In the mountains of Tunbridge, Vermont lies a future retreat center run by Sue Thomas. Sue is deaf, and has been since childhood. This has never stopped her from doing anything she sets her mind to, including becoming an FBI agent who specialized in lip reading conversations of suspects. The TV show "Sue Thomas FBEye" is based on her years with the bureau. Sue, who also now struggles with MS, lives with a young lady named Debra, her personal assistant, as well as an aide dog.

One of Sue's many projects is Operation Silent Night. Each Christmas Eve for the past eight years, she and Debra have led a team of volunteers to Washington DC to give food, blankets, warm clothes and dignity to the people living on the streets. This year we had the blessing to be part of their team.

It started when I offered for my school, Windham Christian Academy, to collect the gloves the team would be bringing to DC. Sue accepted this offer immediately, and invited us to join her. Before we had even decided if we would go, Sue got back to us and said an anonymous donor would pay for our entire trip. I asked if Sue remembered that we were a family of five. Some time passed, and she said we were all invited on this mission, and we would all be paid for!

So on December 23rd, we got in our little car and headed south on I-95. The traffic around New York and northern New Jersey was horrendous! It took us 13 1/2 hours before we arrived at our hotel in Virginia, but we were immediately welcomed by the rest of the team, excited as to most of whom traveled from Ohio. After an orientation and pizza dinner, we went to our suite and went to bed very excited about what the morning would bring.

After Christmas Eve breakfast, we began preparing for our trip into DC. The women prepared sandwiches and 'goodie bags' while the men stuffed backpacks with sweatshirts, flashlights, socks, underwear, rain ponchos, and of course, gloves. Once we were all packed and the bus was loaded, we went to do a little sightseeing before the sun went down. We went to Arlington Cemetery where we saw the changing of the guard and the graves of the three Kennedy brothers. As the sun went down it began to flurry; a special touch for us from Maine who associate snow with Christmas. We were ready to go into the city.

The first homeless person we met was a woman lying in a makeshift bed under a bridge. I approached her with another team member, and she was so grateful for our Christmas gifts. By now the temperature was dropping fast, and we learned later that DC had an unusually low temperature of 16 degrees that night, so the blankets and hot cocoa were especially welcome.

The largest crowd we encountered was on the front steps of one of the Smithsonian museums. I don't know for sure how many people came over to our bus and truck, but we were parked there for quite some time giving backpacks, sandwiches, cocoa, blankets and more. Equally important, we spoke with the people. One man told us how he used to volunteer at a homeless shelter in Seattle, and he understood the good feelings we got helping him. A young woman didn't talk about her background except to say, "I hope my mother gets the Christmas Spirit soon." That was a very telling statement. One man said that it was "the best day ever", and everyone was quick to wish us merry Christmas. We were right where we were supposed to be on Christmas Eve.

While the stereotype of the homeless is that they are alcoholics and / or mentally ill, most of the people we spoke with did not come across as either. Yes, a few people clearly had alcohol on their breath, including three men camped in a tunnel, and yes one woman turned down a blanket because she had her own "magic blanket", but these were the exceptions.

Sue Thomas, of course, knows DC well, and explained that certain parks attract the drug and alcohol addicted homeless, but the people we met on the streets tended to be in different circumstances. She called them the 'hard core' homeless. These were the people who made makeshift tents from tarps, garbage bags, cardboard boxes and umbrellas. One woman, for example, was an immigrant from Eastern Europe (her accent confirmed her story) who married an American man who divorced her within a year.

I'm am so proud of my wife and three daughters, too. Some of my highlights were the opportunities my girls and I had to pray with people before saying good-bye. My wife, Sue, was amazing, too. She led the team in most hugs given and received that night.

We never have had a Christmas Eve quite like this one, and we hope to do it again, soon. After all, Christmas started with a couple, not homeless exactly, but strangers camping out in a barn. Before their child - born in that very stable - turned two years old, they fled to a foreign, and sometimes hostile, country, again homeless, in order to preserve the child's life. This same child grew up to teach us that, when we welcome the homeless we welcome him. There is no one closer to the Spirit of Christmas and the heart of God than the people we spent this Christmas with.

You Blessed Me, Man

We were doing an outreach with several local churches on a city beach in the Boston area this summer. The audience was very diverse in that there were tourists on vacation, local teens enjoying their summer breaks, homeless people taking advantage of the access to public restrooms, many immigrant families, especially Muslim women with their children, and members of gangs, including, we're told, the Cambodian Bloods, all together in one spot.

During one of our afternoon performances, I asked the audience for a large bill with which to do a trick. A twenty-something man covered in 'bling' pulled out a huge wad of cash, peeled off a $100 bill, and handed it to me. After pretending to tear the bill, then vanish the bill, I used it to teach the parable of the lost coin. Eventually I re-appeared the bill and returned it to the man. After the show, he came up to me and said, "You blessed me, man."

Later, some of the local clergy, as well as some of our homeless friends, confirmed what we suspected from the start. This guy was a big time drug dealer in the area.

So, what did it mean when he said, "You blessed me, man"? Was he just being nice? Why did he use the word 'blessed'? Was he trying to use jargon he thought would be most meaningful to us?

Was he trying to manipulate our team somehow? (This seems unlikely, as he was probably carrying more money than the value of everything everyone on the team had combined.) Was he remembering a devout, churchgoing mother or grandmother whom he had long neglected, but our message brought her to mind? Was he letting us know there was a chink in his armor, and the Holy Spirit was slowly calling him to Christ? Was he merely saying he liked the show?

"You blessed me, man." What does it mean when a big time drug dealer says this to you?

Section 3:

POEMS

As well as a couple of routines

Questions

Why do I strive to heal every broken heart;
Do I really believe I'm the only white knight who's been
sent
 to save each damsel in distress?
Why do I hunger to feed every starving child,
And be a father to a fatherless world?
Is it because of God's Spirit flaring up in my soul,
Or simply to boost my fragile male ego;
Will I rejoice when His Kingdom has come to earth
Or grieve because there are no kingdoms left to conquer?

Why do I preach on every soapbox and stage;
Why must I always be liked?
Why do I play to the crowd every scene?
Why can't I let a single windmill stand unchallenged?
Do I want to see the final dragon's head on the wall,
Or will I weep when there's none left to fight?
Is it because of God's Spirit flaring up in my soul,
Or simply to boost my fragile male ego;
Will I rejoice when His Kingdom has come to earth
Or grieve because there are no kingdoms left to conquer?

Why do I fixate on what my legacy will be;
Can't the hope of eternity be sufficient?
Can I honestly say my reason for living
is to worship and enjoy my Creator;
Or is my unspoken,
 unacknowledged,
unflattering, motivation
to prove self-significance and self-worth?
If so, what does that say about my soul?

Psalm 23 for Pessimists

The Lord is your Shepherd

Shepherds give me the willeys! Those long robes and head coverings and big, bushy beards. It's like they're in a disguise or something.

I'll make you lie down in green pastures.

Now there's a great idea. I'll be covered with ticks for the rest of the day!

I'll lead you beside still waters.

I didn't even pack my swim suit! Don't for a minute think you'll get me to go skinny dipping! And that water's probably full of leaches. That's all I need; dozens of blood sucking leaches all over my naked body.

I'll lead you in paths of righteousness

So now we're going hiking! With all the blood loss from the ticks and the leaches, I'll be lucky to make it ten steps. I don't have a water bottle, I'm wearing the wrong shoes, and I bet this path of yours has lousy cell reception. If I fall and twist my ankle because of my bad shoes, I won't be able to call 911, and I'll probably die of dehydration before the EMT's can find me and airlift me to a hospital!

Even though we walk through the valley of the shadow of death

What did I tell you!

I am with you, my rod and my staff will comfort you.

That's another thing. It's bad enough you're dressed in that sketchy shepherd suit; do you have to carry weapons, too?

I prepare a table before you...

At least remember that I have strawberry allergies. Give me anything with strawberries and my throat will tighten up and I'll die of anaphylactic shock.

In the presence of your enemies

Way to add insult to injury

I'll anoint your head with oil

It takes days to rinse that stuff out of my hair.

Your cup runs over

Great! So I'm gonna spill my coffee again today!

Surely goodness and mercy will follow you all the days of your life

Are you telling me that some stalkers named Shirley and Mercy are tailing me everywhere I go?

And you shall dwell in the house of the Lord forever.

Let me get this straight. I'll survive the Creepy shepherd and his friends Shirley and Mercy; I'll endure infestations of ticks and leaches, food poisoning and wandering aimlessly on some wilderness path only to get into a lifetime mortgage I'll never get out of? Just my luck!

Amen

Whatever!

Beautiful Girl

Beautiful girl; Daughter of the heavens.
Aching to smile; surrendered to tears.
Didn't she read the medical journals, circa 1872?

"Blood-letting has been determined to have no healing benefits."

But that's what she does …
since she can't afford liposuction ;

Or doesn't like the taste of her own vomit;

Or she's realized she'll never look remotely like Miley Cyrus; even with her clothes on.

"Just one more slash; It calms you;"

It does.

That's the oxymoron, the sinister miracle of it all.

It does.

It does.

Confusion clears, rage relaxes, peace prevails.

Wounding herself for her unholy trinity of transgressions:

anxiety, depression and lonliness.

Until that day -

In the emergency room; Or in her empty apartment;
Or in her dorm when her roommate's gone for the
weekend;

And her forearm's wrapped in humid crimson bandages -

Finally she imagines - Determined it's a lie, still dreaming
that it's true -

Maybe there's no cleansing in her blood, only the incurable
DNA of a fallen race,

Perhaps broken glass is no crown of thorns
Perhaps razor blades make poor nails that will never hold
her scarred wrists to the Cross of self-redemption.

My darling, by your own stripes you'll die.

By His stripes you're healed.

Try to imagine.

Try to believe.

For Miley, Michael, Lindsey, all the Bulimic Beauty Queens and the Family in Church Who Seem to Have Their S#!t Together

It looked like a bassinette at first. Instead of a cradle, however, it was a pedestal that her daddy constantly placed her on. Then there was a rush of excitement and pride as the pedestal grew skyward; but as it got taller and narrower it became clear that there was no way off without hurling herself to her death. A pedestal, it seems, is just a different kind of prison cell.

He streaked through the water and was honored by the entire world with medals and praises. One after another, the gold discs were placed over his neck to the tune of his anthem and the adoration of his fans. But medals aren't buoyant. As the medal count grew, they pulled him down, deeper and deeper beneath the surface. Fighting the weight that's pulling him down, he thrashes to the surface gasping for breath. But he's quick to go down again. Medals, it seems, are just another millstone around the neck if one is already drowning.

At first the articles were reviews; "An exceptionally gifted child," "Brilliant", "Talented beyond her years". Then the ink dried for a season. New headlines appeared with a decidedly different tone: "Shoplifting", "Drugs", "Jail".
With time and pushy parents, the good reviews returned, but with all the same gossip interspersed. She clipped them all and saved them in her scrap book and on her fridge. But in the end, all those accolades just make for a longer entry on the obituary page.

Tiara perched on her big hair, Vaseline toothed and slender, she was awarded her first trophy. As she grew taller, the trophies did too; double handled loving cups filled with champagne so sweet she couldn't detect the arsenic lacing every sip. Writhing on the floor as she vomited out her life… beauty lost years ago.

Dressed in their Sunday best, smiles that could light up Heaven itself, singing with the voices of angels, quoting chapter and verse. "If only we could be like that family." Yet every greeting of peace feels like a dementor's kiss, and every pat on the back is another chisel blow, shaping them into objects of worship they were never intended to be. Behind the veil, they fight, doubt, grieve, ache…

Gods of wood will burn, gods of stone will crumble, and gods of flesh and blood will die and rot.

But Lord, have mercy on those who sculpt these idols.

Raggedy Anne

Raggedy Anne showed up at school today
Finding Barbies, again, at each turn,
The plastic girls mock Anne's dowdiness,
Yet the teachers still expect her to learn.

With flaming red hair and an apron
She should stand out as not just a clone.
Yet she spends every school day unnoticed
And eternal lunch breaks eating alone.

Herds of young men (or is it young Ken)
Turn empty heads toward the Barbies and stare
At their disproportionate PVC bodies,
And waist length nylon hair.

When Raggedy walks down the hallway
The Kens laugh at her pigtails and size
And the boys who were raised to know better
Say nothing, diverting their eyes.

But the doll maker knows rags and cotton
Are warmer than stiff, rigid plastic
And aprons absorb more secrets and tears
Than any cold, hard, plastic stick

As for the young men (or is it young Ken)
So arrogantly loud in the hall,
The doll makers knows, if you'd just sneak a peek,
You'd see they're not really men at all.

Matthew 25:42

An elderly man, whose home was the street
Asked the Episcopalians for something to eat,
But they offered the homeless man nothing to eat;
They were too busy preparing to go on retreat.
They said, "Go see the Catholics when they get out of mass;
"Yes, go see the Catholics; they're the ones with the cash."

But the Catholics offered him nothing at all.
They were saving their pennies for a new parish hall.
They said, "Why don't you go give the Baptists a call.
"They might just help, being 'fundies' after all."
But the Baptist said they had nothing to share;
They just said, "Get a job and go cut your hair.
Or, "see the Methodist church, those old bleeding hearts;
"Yes the Methodist church is the place you should start."

At the Methodist church, the man still wasn't served.
The food in their kitchen had all been reserved
For the youth group picnic and the ladies' lunch,
The singles mixer and the senior brunch.
The Lutherans also gave him no food that day
And the Pentecostals turned him away.
But the truth is, we'll meet this homeless man some day
and we'll have to explain why we turned Him away.

The Lord's Day in the Park

I caught your eye today,
but you quickly looked away,
and threw bread out on the pond and on the grass.
The pigeons at your feet,
Took all that they could eat,
While my last meal was taken from the trash.

You pretended not to see,
But you sneaked a look at me.
You didn't say a word, you only sneered.
You do not know my name,
And you showed no sign of shame,
When your children pointed, laughed at me and jeered.

You think it's a disgrace;
You used to like this place,
"But now'" you say, "There's more bums here every day."
"They're dirty and they smell,
"This park has gone to hell."
You wonder why you bother to even stay.

You throw the squirrels the crust,
While my eyes search through the dust;
But the bread's all gone; My hope once more deflated.
While hunger weakens me,
The final irony
Is that it's in My image you have been created.

Reruns

I've never learned my neighbor's name,
Now let me tell you who's to blame:
Professor, Gilligan and Skipper,
Gentle Ben, Lassie, Flipper,
Chrissy, Janet, and Jack Tripper,
Betty, Wilma, Barney, Fred,
Trigger, Silver, Mr. Ed,
Helen Roper, Mr. Furley,
Lucy, Ethel, Laverne and Shirley,
Fred Sanford, LaMont and Grady,
Greg, Peter and Bobby Brady.

While my neighbors travel life's rough road
I'll watch another episode.
Checking in on Lou Grant,
Underdog and Atom Ant,
Mary Richards, Rhoda, Phyllis,
Mr. Drummond, Arnold, Willis,
Maynard Krebs and Dobie Gillis,
Fonzie, Richie, Mr. C,
Andy, Opie and Aunt Bea,
Urkel, Screech, Lenny, Squiggy,
Kermit, Fozie and Miss Piggy,
Colonel Hogan, and Klink, too,
Captains Kirk and Kangaroo,

My neighborhood might need a hand,
But I reside in TV land,
With Mister Rogers, Magoo and Spock,
Highway to Heaven's where I walk.
Even Gomer Pyle and Barney Fife
Know that reruns have eternal life.

Untitled Poem by our Second Daughter, Naomi

Fear is seductive
His hot,
stinging breath
dances upon my mouth
familiar, warm and
out of reach
calling me to come in
closer, closer.
His firm, strong hand
placed on my lower back
draws me into him.
I take a step
and then another.
My body presses against his
and his lips burn me
as he kisses my forehead lightly,
leaving a strange feeling
an empty feeling
where his lips touched.
Then he tilts my chin up
and kisses me.
His tongue scorches my mouth
burns my lips
blisters my tongue.
I cry out in pain
and try to pull away,
too late.
His strong, restricting arms
wrap around me
capturing me in his painful embrace.
The fire's unbearable

I'm ready to die
My clothes burn off
then he drops me.
I stand there
naked and exposed to him.
Every imperfection and burn
is exposed.
Intimacy and desire
replaced with confusion
"I thought you loved me"
"I don't love you, my dear"
he said in his sweetest voice
"I NEED you.
so come back...
and I'll care for you.
Feed me
and I'll be there for you"
He holds his arms out
waiting for my response.
I turn to walk away
but something holds me back
where once stood a man named Fear
is now an infant.
I pick him up.
I cuddle him.
And I carry him home.
After all,
he's just a helpless babe,
right?

Judgement Day: A Skit

JESUS: When the Son of Man comes in His glory, and all His angels with Him, He shall sit on His glorious throne, and He will separate the people one from another as a shepherd separates the sheep from the goats.

ME: So this is it. This is the day you open up the Book of Life, and find MY name. Go ahead, I'm ready.

JESUS: I was hungry, and you gave me nothing to eat. I was thirsty and you gave me nothing to drink.

ME: Uh, Lord, are you still sore about that? You need to let this go. You remember the problem. That weekend I was invited to be part of the church's soup kitchen ministry was the same weekend the Christian TV network was having a Left Behind marathon. I wanted to understand everything there was to know about your Judgment Day. What could feeding the homeless possibly have to do with Judgment Day?

JESUS: I was naked, and you did not clothe me.

ME: Are you referring to the fund raiser for the poor in Central America. I wanted to donate, you know, but money was tight right then.

I didn't have enough for that AND my tattoo. Want me to show you my tattoo... uh, maybe not. But it's OK, 'cause it's a Christian tattoo. It's a dove with the reference.... Leviticus 19:35. That's the one that says... Uh, it talks about, um... it's the verse about, uh, God or something. You should know, you wrote it! Anyway, it's an expensive tattoo, and I couldn't afford both.

JESUS: I was a stranger and you did not invite me in.

ME: Yeah, I remember that teen in our church who needed to get out of his home for a while. Sure, we could have let him stay with us, but it's risky letting someone like him into your house. What if he stole my iPod, or my laptop, or even my solid gold cross necklace with diamond chips on each end? How could I witness effectively if he had stolen my solid gold cross necklace with diamond chips on each end?

JESUS: I was sick and in prison and you did not visit me.

ME: Lord, come on now. We've been over this and over this. That missions trip to the AIDS orphanage in Africa was very poorly timed. It fell at the same time as Glenn Beck's big rally in Washington DC. Who could possibly represent You better to the world than Glenn Beck. It didn't hurt that Sarah Palin was there, too. Remember when she looked into the TV camera and winked right at me! Uh... where were we? Oh, right, hi Lord.

JESUS: I was hooked on drugs, and you watched the addiction kill me; I was an unborn child, and you let me get aborted; I was in a cult, and you let me die believing a lie.

ME: Now Lord, I happen to know this passage of Scripture you're quoting; I memorized it in Sunday School. And there's not a single reference to abortion, drugs or cults. You shouldn't put your own interpretation into the Scriptures like that! Have you been reading the Message?

JESUS: Depart from me, I never knew you.

ME: Now come on, Lord. Remember all those weekends I gave up for retreats; the money I spent on Christian concerts. And it wasn't all Christian rock, either. I even had some CDs by George Beverly Shea.

(JESUS SHAKES HEAD 'NO')

ME: Not even for George Beverly Shea... I should have known a man named Beverly was suspect! Well what about my car? Remember my 'Honk if you Love Jesus' bumper sticker and my 'Psalm 23' vanity license plate? What could be godlier than a vanity license plate? Send someone down there to bring up my car. Send an angel like Gabriel or Michael or Michael Landon,

JESUS: Depart from me, I never knew you.

ME: Hey, but...

JESUS: Depart from me, I never knew you! And these shall go away into eternal punishment, and the righteous into eternal life.

Letters to Soo: A skit

In the 80's there was a ministry called 'Slavic Gospel Association', through which believers in the West could write letters of encouragement to oppressed believers in the communist bloc. This concept inspired the following skit, which addresses how out of touch many American Christians are to what it really means to lay down our lives for our faith.

I wrote this skit years ago and it has never been performed. I picture an actor on either side of the stage alternately writing these letters as they speak what they're writing aloud.

Dear Soo Dok-Ling,

My name is Richard Davis, and I got your name from the Chinese – American Gospel Association. It is the desire of my wife, Vivian and me to encourage you as you struggle living out your faith in a communist country. Speaking of struggles, our 12 year old daughter, Lynn, came home yesterday with the ugliest yellow nail polish. What will the elders at First Community Church think if we let her wear something like that!

Our family is praying for you.

Sincerely,

The Davis's

Dear Mr. Davis,

Thank you for the letter and prayers. I, too, was married, but my husband, a pastor, has been missing for several months, now. He was very prominent in the underground church here in China, so there is little reason to think I'll see him again soon. My hope now is for when I see him in eternity. My new baby son, Jin-Woo, looks just like him.

In spite of our trials, our fellowship continues to meet frequently, usually in homes. Although we are always concerned about government officials infiltrating our meetings, it is always a joy to worship with other brothers and sisters.

In Jesus,

Soo Dok-Ling

Dear Soo,

I was very interested in reading about your home fellowship meetings. Our church, too, has started home cell group meetings every Wednesday night.

Viv and I haven't been attending, as the closest one is a good 20 minute drive away. Not only that, but as much as our pastor stresses that they shouldn't last over 90 minutes, I hear they often go until at least 8:30! It's just not worth it.

Our Sunday service is nice, though. I just wish the church governing board wasn't so concerned with the fuel bill. The last few Sundays have been rather chilly.

Your brother in Christ,

Richard Davis

Dear Brother Richard,

Thank you for writing again so quickly. My English skills are weak, so I do not understand 'fuel bills' or 'governing board'. But I do know what you mean by cold services. Sometimes, when we suspect the government may try to break up one of our meetings, we meet secretly in the woods. Of course, the love of Christ and fellow believers keeps me from being overwhelmed by the chill, but sometimes poor little Jin cries so hard we fear the police will find us as we secretly worship in the darkness. We praise God for His protection to this point.

In Christ,

Soo Dok-Ling

Dear Soo,

I can sure relate to your story of how little Jin disrupts church. A few weeks ago, Lynn wore a dreadful looking mini skirt and leggings to church.

Actually, Viv and I thought she looked okay, but some of the deaconesses clearly didn't approve.

Last night Viv and I went to a Chinese restaurant. We blew fifty bucks! You people sure eat well.

Your brother in Christ,

Richard

Dear Richard,

Again, I ask for forgiveness for my poor English. I do not understand 'blew fifty bucks', and I do not know what a mini skirt and leggings are.

Yes, my people have been eating well this year. We praise the Lord for a wonderful harvest in our village. Most families have been able to eat two full meals every day! I pray that such extravagance does not cause us to take our eyes off of Jesus. I especially rejoice because we have a family in our church whose little boy was born very handicapped. The prosperity of this harvest has allowed him to live longer than anyone expected. He is a true living miracle.

Love in Christ,

Soo Dok-Ling

My Dear Sister in Christ,

I can relate to the family in your church that has a child with a handicap. I'm quite sure our younger child has a learning disability. His grades are nothing like his older sister's. The school psychologist and our pediatrician both say he's normal, but why else would a child of ours be getting B's and C's on his report cards? Please pray that he is found eligible for services as a disabled child soon.

Your American Brother,

Richard

Dear Brother in Christ,

My English is obviously very poor. Your letter sounded to me, in my ignorance, as if you *wanted* your child to be found with a disability. Obviously I misunderstood, as that would make no sense at all.

The Chinese government has been cracking down on unapproved churches, at least in our region. As I hear of homes being burned and pastors being arrested, I desire more every day to see my Jesus return for His bride, the church. Hopefully soon.

In Him,

Soo Dok-Ling

Dear Soo,

I am sorry to hear about the treatment of Christians in your region of China. I, too, continue to look toward the clouds, as each day here also has its share of trials. For example, just this week our refrigerator broke down, and I got a flat tire coming home from work. Then, to top it all off, our cable went out for five hours! I truly believe we are living in the end times.

Sincerely,

Richard

Dear Mr. Davis and Family,

I will not tell you my name, as I fear for my safety and that of my family. It is enough to say we have a mutual friend in Soo Dok-Ling. As of a few days ago, she and baby Jin-Woo have been missing. Please do not try to write back, as that could jeopardize the safety of many other believers. Pray for us and we will pray for you. 'To live is Christ, and to die is gain.'

-A friend

(Richard folds letter, pauses, then picks up remote and turns on TV)

How Can I Be Wrong

Make no mistake, I believe in creation, and I am uncompromisingly pro-life, but extreme politics is not how the Kingdom of God was ever meant to expand. It is with that in mind that I wrote the following:

Alaska has the cutest gov'nor any state has ever seen.
Palin's the hottest politician since Esther the Old Testament Queen.
And I'll never forget that evening when she winked at me through my TV screen.
Tell me, how can I be wrong when I'm the religious right?

Nothing is more patriotic than toting a pistol or two.
America's West was settled by blasting Cherokee, Blackfoot and Sioux,
And if Jesus had been here incarnate, He'd have wasted some savages, too.
Tell me, how can I be wrong when I'm the religious right?

I believe in God the Creator; I'm a special jewel in His crown.
I reject evolution completely, Darwin's a heretic clown.
Every day I thank God for nature, now let's get busy cutting it down.
Tell me, how can I be wrong when I'm the religious right?

At least once a month you'll find me at an overpriced weekend retreat.
I attend Michael W's concerts; tickets cost forty bucks per seat,
But I don't give to the poor or the homeless,

They need to get jobs and get off my street.
Tell me, how can I be wrong when I'm the religious right?

Children should all have a nice home, led by one husband and wife.
Every time there comes an election, you can be sure I'll be voting pro-life.
But don't talk to me 'bout adopting, that's too big a sacrifice.
Tell me, how can I be wrong, when I'm the religious right?

I pray for the gays and the perverts, immigrants from Sudan and Iraq.
I pray for the whores and their babies, born addicted to liquor and crack.
I ask God to bless them and heal them, and keep them off of my cul-de-sac.
Tell me, how can I be wrong when I'm the religious right?

JESUS LOVES THE CHILDREN: A Skit

(Inspired by Simon and Garfunkel's "Silent Night / the 7:00 News")

Singer: "Jesus loves the little children...'

Reporter: The Department of Human Services has released its latest report on poverty in this state, and the numbers are not encouraging. 25% of all children living in this state are below the poverty level.

Singer: "All the children of the world..."

Reporter: The United Nations reports that 25,000 children have died of hunger related issues again this year."

Singer: "Red brown yellow black and white..."

Reporter: In Thailand today there was an explosion in a factory where 210 children were forced into slave labor against their wills. Rescuers continue to search for survivors.

Singer: "They are precious in his sight; Jesus loves the little children of the world"

Reporter: Once again a local clergyman has been taken in for questioning regarding accusations of child abuse

Singer: "Jesus loves the little children of the world"

Reporter: This year marks the 40th anniversary of the legalization of abortion in this country. In that time, over 50,000,000 abortions have been performed.

Singer: "Jesus loves the little children of the world."

Old Paul

When I was a 16 year old counselor in training at a Vermont summer camp, we used to walk into town on our days off. One day we saw an old guy in his driveway, and we waved to him. He struck up a conversation with us, and we went inside. We were stupid kids, but fortunately old Paul wasn't looking for trouble, just a break in his loneliness, boredom and drunkenness that he lived in day after day. We went back a couple other times, and I've often wondered what his story was and how it ended.

Moths swarm around old Paul's porch light;
Mosquitos investigate his screens;
Spider webs cover all his windows,
And cobwebs cover all his dreams.

There's cans of baked beans in his cupboard,
His glass has a few more sips of gin.
A cigarette again has turned to ashes
Like the spark that once had burned within.

Paul's got an ex-wife out in Denver;
A second one moved up to Montreal.
His five kids live up and down the east coast,
But none of them ever care to call.

Of course, there's still Bill from the tool shop,
He still lives in his house across the town.
But ever since the two of them retired
Bill never seems to want to come around.
It seems the smell of dust and squalor,
And the smell of stale tobacco smoke,

The smell of lack of hope and hygiene
Make Bill feel like he wants to cry or choke.
Besides, Bill still has his Nancy,
they've been married for 47 years.
And old Paul has a little gin left,
And a soul so dry he has no more tears.

Paul allows himself to see some promise
In each new bottle he walks to town and buys.
But again, the summer sun is setting,
And again, his bottle quickly dries.
He falls asleep at his kitchen table,
As loneliness and gin take their toll.
One wonders which vessel is more empty,
His bottle on the floor or his hollow soul?

The moths still swarm around the porch light,
Mosquitos still investigate his screens.
Spiders spin additions to their webbed homes,
They continue to pursue their simple dreams.
Though sleeping now, Paul does no dreaming,
Dreams he once had have slowly passed,
Up to Montreal and out to Denver,
And in the bottom of another empty glass.

Innocent Love

Forty years old; a wife and two kids
His hair's turning gray as his father's hair did.
His kids aren't perfect, like he dreamt they would be,
and his wife's not as cute as the wives on TV.
Now he wants to go back to what never was,
He longs for lost youth and innocent love.
His teens were no picnic, but his memories lie.
He longs to go back so he decided to try
to return to a time that just never was;
To return to a time of innocent love.

Twenty two years old. She never knew her old man,
So she learned to act tough as only a victim can.
No longer a virgin since she turned fifteen;
She searched for someone to be the dad of her dreams.
Though she'll never speak it, deep in her heart,
She's looking for someone to play Daddy's part.
She wants to experience what never was:
A daughter and father and innocent love.

They met in a bar room drinking some beers
In hopes they would wash away all their tears.
Two lonely strangers walked out of the bar
Though they just barely met, she got into his car.
He got a hotel room hoping not to be seen;
In hopes she'd fill his middle aged dreams.

But now he's more lonely then he'd been before,
And she's given herself to be used once more.
Trying to get back to what never was
Isn't the road to innocent love.
In the Garden of Eden innocence was lost;
Now innocent love is only found at the Cross.

Little Chrissy Christian
(A story I've told for years.)

This is a story about a Christian family. In fact, that's their name, the Christian family. There's Mommy Christian, Daddy Christian, and their precious little daughter, Chrissy Christian. Chrissy's about three years old, and she's playing on the floor with her Barbies. It's OK; they're Christian Barbies... each one has a dove tattooed on her hip. Little Chrissy is having her Barbies raise their hands in the air while she sings 'Jesus Loves Me'. This blesses Mommy Christian's heart, so she picks Chrissy up, sets her in her lap, and asks, "Do you want to ask Jesus to live in your heart?"

Of course, Chrissy has no idea how a big man like Jesus can come live inside her heart, but she does know that sitting in Mommy's lap is a lot more comfortable than on the cold floor, so she says, "Sure, Mommy."

Mommy Christian says, "Repeat this prayer." Mommy says a few words, Chrissy repeats them; Mommy says a few more words, Chrissy repeats them, and, praise God, little Chrissy Christian is saved and on her way to Heaven.

Then Chrissy becomes a teenager, and meets a boy... Troy. Troy the Boy. Troy is a lifeguard at the beach Chrissy frequents, and they have fallen madly in love, because, after all, he's seen her in her bikini! It's OK, it's a Christian bikini. There's a dove embroidered on the behind.

Chrissy rushes home and tells Mommy and Daddy Christian that she's in love. Daddy Christian asks, "Is he a Christian?' And Chrissy says, "Ummmm, I don't know. It never came up."

Daddy Christian smiles a knowing smile and says, "Invite the boy over for supper."

The next day, Troy shows up at the house. Daddy gives him a hearty hand shake and says, "Son, if you're going to date my daughter, you need to accept Jesus into your heart." Troy has no idea what this means, but he sure wants to stay with Chrissy. So he says, "OK."

Daddy says, "Repeat this prayer." Daddy says a few words, Troy repeats them, Daddy says a few more words and Troy repeats them. Praise God, Troy is saved, and now it's OK for the young couple to date.

Like all good 'Christian' teens, they get married right out of high school so as not to fall, or jump, into temptation... But then, in three, or five, or ten years, people are wondering why she's sleeping around, or why he's beating her, or why their hearts have simply grown cold to each other, and it's because they never really had what people told them they had... they never really had what *they* thought they had.

We do young people a disservice when we cheapen the Gospel to an echoed prayer, especially without adequate explanation and true conviction of sins. Worse, it's an offense to the Gospel itself. Jesus died for more than just empty, token words. He died to redeem our every thought, word, belief and action. He calls us to total surrender to Him, and to cling completely to His grace alone when we fall short. Anything less is not Christianity according to Jesus.

Section 4

THE POTTERY CONTEMPLATES THE POTTER

Thoughts on God, Life and Scripture

Risks, Righteousness, and the Illusion of Safety

Being a juggler is all about taking risks. Being a juggler who performs rather than just juggles for recreation is even more so. Every toss is a possible mistake. My life would feel a lot more 'safe' if I stuck to routines I've been performing successfully for years... or if I only juggled for fun and fitness... or if I just watched other jugglers on TV and never actually tried it myself...

In His book 'Wild Goose Chase', which I highly recommend, author Mark Batterson states, "Quit living as if the purpose of life is to arrive safely at death." This goes completely against much of the conventional wisdom that humankind has always followed. But for a follower of Jesus, this statement should be both profound and convicting. First, we need to acknowledge the fact that all attempts at absolute safety are illusions. While it's true that God would not have us live recklessly, it's also true that there are no guarantees of safety, ever. What, for example, conjures up a picture of peace and tranquility more than an Amish schoolhouse? Yet one such school was the site of mass murder just a few years ago. A few years earlier, Cassie Burnell arrived safely at Columbine High School, and was quietly studying in the library, when suddenly she became a martyr for her faith at the hands of two armed classmates. Planes can crash, houses can burn, lightning can strike, illusions of security can be shattered.

Now please don't misunderstand me, God has made us stewards of our lives and the lives of those in our care: children, elderly parents, students, etc. We must take good care of them. As Steve Camp said, "To live dangerously is not to live recklessly but righteously." So when something is RIGHT, we must do it uncompromisingly, fearlessly, or, perhaps, in spite of our fears. In other words, we must forgive without restraint, give without holding back, speak without watering down the truth, go on that mission trip without all the comforts of a tourist, visit the sick and imprisoned without judgement, confront sin without compromise, and open the most private places in our hearts to the Holy Spirit without excuse.

"Perfect love casts out all fear," Scripture says. I want to do more with the life Jesus has given me than simple live safely until I die.

Is God Pragmatic?

Pragmatism is defined as: "An approach that assesses the truth of meaning of theories or beliefs in terms of the success of their practical application." In other words, pragmatism says something is true if it works. How often, when working with teens, talking to incarcerated persons, or even in my own moments of vulnerability, do I hear, "I tried Jesus (or prayer, or doing what's right, etc.) and it didn't work." How do Christians come to grips with that, when, in truth, doing things God's way often doesn't seem to 'work'?

First of all, we need to define what it means to 'work'. We need to ask, "What is God's definition of success?" Romans 5 tells us that suffering leads to perseverance, which leads to character, which leads to hope. God's definition of success, then, isn't an absence of suffering or difficulties, but a hope that doesn't fail. But, in truth, that kind of hope *only* comes as a result of suffering. To quote William Penn, "No pain, no palm; no thorn, no throne; no gall, no glory; no cross, no crown."

We also need to consider God's eternal perspective. True success, as defined by God, is very different from what we often call immediate success. Did Joseph, in the Old Testament, see how things were working out when he was buried in a ditch in the wilderness by his jealous brothers? It took many years before that incident came to 'work out' in the saving of the entire Hebrew race.

God is in no rush. In fact, that same passage in Romans 5 seems to imply that there will usually be a significant passage of time between the trial and the resolution to the trial that leads to hope. The word perseverance implies a long time of suffering. By definition, persevering for five minutes, or five hours or five days isn't really persevering at all.

Is God pragmatic? That depends on whether or not we let God define 'success', or if we accept our culture's definition. "All things work together for good to those who love the Lord and are called according to His purpose."

Revelation 3: 15 – 16

"I know your deeds, that you are neither cold nor hot. I wish you were either one or the other!   So, because you are lukewarm-- neither hot nor cold--I am about to spit you out of my mouth." – Revelation 3:15 – 16

I've always found it interesting that God would rather we be cold than lukewarm. Obviously, He would prefer we were hot, on fire in our faith, following Him with a burning passion, than to be putting on a lukewarm façade of faith. But do we really grasp that He also would prefer we were stone cold, dead in our sinful deeds, than to be lukewarm? This seems so counterintuitive, but it's right there in black and white.

What does this mean in practical terms? It means, if our kids go to youth retreats, but their motivation is simply to get away from their parents, God would rather they sneaked off for the weekend with their friends. Maybe their parents would prefer they are safe and lukewarm on retreat, but God prefers even ice coldness to lukewarmness.

It means, if we flock to our 'Christian concerts' in order to be entertained by religious celebrities, God would prefer we were ice cold, and perhaps attending the latest concert by Lady GaGa. It means, if we support political candidates for our own comfort and prosperity rather than the ones who support biblical values of justice, truth and integrity, God would prefer we don't vote at all.

Actually, I think I may be understating it when I say 'God would prefer...' God says it in a much stronger way: "I am about to spew you out of my mouth."

When we are lukewarm in our walk of faith, which is often typified by doing 'Christian' things with selfish or worldly motivation, it makes God puke. Middle of the road faith makes God sick. At least someone who is cold toward God isn't fooling anyone. Lukewarm faith can fool church members, clergy, family, and, usually even the person whose heart is lukewarm himself. But it never fools God.

"I know your deeds, that you are neither hot nor cold..."

Wait
(journal entry, 4/22/2011)

Today is Good Friday. Easter is in two days, and the season of Lent is coming to an end. I was reminded recently that Lent is a season, like Advent, that emphasizes waiting patiently. We wait to resume the pleasures of life we have willingly given up for a season. We wait for the celebration of Christ's resurrection. We wait for spring-like weather. (As recently as yesterday, here in Maine there were still snow flurries.) We wait like the first group of believers who waited three days, still unclear on what was going to happen now that their Master had been executed. And Thomas, the biggest doubter in the group, waited an additional week before he saw the resurrected Messiah face to face.

It seems God uses those who are willing to wait patiently, even if we have no idea how things will get resolved. Old Testament Joseph was in exile for 20 years before he caught a glimpse of what God was really up to. Noah waited 40 days for the rain to stop. Abraham waited until he was 100 to have the son he was promised. Jesus, God With Us, waited 30 years before He started His public ministry. The disciples waited for weeks after the ascension of Christ before the Holy Spirit was poured out on them at Pentecost. The world waited for centuries between the prophecies of the coming of the Messiah and that first Christmas.

To follow the Lord is often to wait. Of course, it is against our nature to wait, and it is very much against our current first world culture to wait. We have drive-through restaurants, pharmacies, and bank windows. We have promises of instant relief for headaches, and instant weight loss plans. We have high speed internet and instant deposit pay checks. But, as the love of money is the root of all evil, the distain for waiting is the root of a lot of bad decisions. Thieves won't wait to earn the things they desire so badly, so they steal. Impulsive young people won't wait to have sexual relationships, and end up with pregnancies they're unprepared for. Eager couples won't wait for a longer courtship, so they marry quickly, and our divorce rate continues to sky rocket. On and on it goes.

Why does God want us to wait? The book of Romans tells us that suffering leads to perseverance, which leads to character, which leads to hope. God's not all that concerned that we get what we want. He's concerned that we become the kind of person He intended us to be. That takes time. We have to wait.

I remember taking my daughters to a hockey game, and the whole audience came to its feet to cheer on a fight that ended with a player being removed by EMTs and blood stains seeping into the ice. It made me nauseous when I realized I was among those cheering, and my girls were watching not just the assault, but my example. I can try to explain it away a lot of different ways, but in the end, I was sinning when I was cheering on this hideous act of violence.

Psalm 11:5 tells us that the Lord's "soul hates the lover of violence". Notice that it does not say He "loves the sinner and hates the sin", a cliché we are often taught in Sunday school. *He hates the lover of violence.* Notice, too, that it says God's *soul* hates the lover of violence. This hate comes from the deepest, most intimate part of God: His soul. This certainly should cause believers to pause and reflect. Does 'hate' mean now what it meant then? Does God both love and hate the lovers of violence simultaneously? I imagine an entire course in seminary could be taught on this topic.

Although my daughter, Jo, has finished her freshman year at Nyack Bible College, she hasn't apparently taken "God's Hatred 101" yet. But she did tell me of an interesting exchange with one professor:

When she told the teacher that she did her high school senior speech on a biblical view of pacifism, the professor replied, "You went to a Christian school, didn't you? Don't they usually steer all their graduates toward the military?" This would be an unfortunate stereotype, if it wasn't true. And while I don't by any means think all who serve in the military are lovers of violence, I know that many of these Christian high school students talk a lot more about killing 'the SOBs' than they do the love and grace of God. On the other hand, my dad served in WWII, and I'm very proud of him. He was not a lover of violence by any stretch of the imagination, but he saw WWII as an unfortunate necessity.

Certainly, for Christians, Augustine's Just War Theory allows for my dad's convictions. Unfortunately, Augustine's theory- the definitive statement about Christianity and warfare- is scarcely known to baby boom era American believers. Instead, we have Christians whose attitude is, like Noel Paul Stookey sings:

"Though we're pastorally encouraged to love them as we pray,
We'll evidently take a break to blow them all away."

But, just-warfare aside, Christians seem strangely accepting of violence. Chuck Norris is a huge hero to evangelical youth. And let's be honest, we watch his shows and movies for the fighting, period. It's certainly not his acting ability that pulls us in! I read an article recently on 'Christian' mixed martial arts, and evangelical karate has been around for years. Christian moshing is as commonplace at 'Gospel' concerts as tacky evangelical tee shirts. A popular televangelist (false prophet?) advocates the assassination of Hugo Chavez, and the religious right is one of the NRA's biggest supporters. Then there's the darling of the religious right agenda (cult theology ignored) who has said, "I'm thinking about killing Michael Moore, and I'm wondering if I could kill him myself, or if I would need to hire somebody to do it. ... No, I think I could. I think he could be looking me in the eye, you know, and I could just be choking the life out."

So what do we do with Psalm 11:5? "His soul hates the lover of violence?" What do we do with all the many more verses about turning the other cheek, being a peace maker, and having a spirit of peace and self-control? We either need to take a lot of white out to our Bibles, or we need to turn off the reruns of "Walker, Texas Ranger", stop listening to self-appointed commentators on FOX and TBN who advocate assassinations and murder, and turn our eyes on the Prince of Peace. May we never be a people so wrapped up in our politics and entertainment, that we become lovers of violence, hated by God.

I Kings 19

First Kings 19: 11 - 18 tells the story of Elijah seeking the Lord's direction. In part, it goes like this: "Now there was a great wind, so strong it split mountains... but the Lord was not in the wind... and after the wind, an earthquake, but the Lord was not in the earthquake; and after the earthquake, a fire, but the Lord was not in the fire; and after the fire a sheer silence..." The story goes on to tell how the Lord was in the silence, and Elijah heard the soft voice of the Lord.

I've been thinking about this passage a lot lately. We seem to have accepted as normal, even worthy in our church culture, to crave the gale force wind-earthquake-fire- experiences and miss the voice of the Lord. We're drawn to glitz, power and celebrity. Meanwhile, regular church attendance is dropping among professing Christians, and we have a church culture of biblical illiterates and spiritual babies.

When I was principal of a small Christian school in rural Maine, I always resisted the temptation to have what is known as 'Spiritual Emphasis Week'. This is a week of school set aside for special services with (inevitably 'cool') youth speakers to minister to the students who the teachers had been working with all year long.

My belief is that every week should be spiritual emphasis week, and who better to do it than the adults who have an ongoing relationship with the kids? I also refused to have middle school or high school retreats for the same reason. I did have annual ministry trips of 4 or 5 days chaperoned by teachers and parents- again the people who really knew the kids- working alongside them in a new and challenging setting.

I must admit I feel like a hypocrite saying this, as the Supreme Court Jesters have been utilized for spiritual emphasis weeks twice in one of the longest running Christian schools in the world in Quito, Ecuador. We have also been utilized in countless retreats as well. I cannot explain away this contradiction; all I can do is recognize it and acknowledge it.

I also acknowledge that people in general, and young people especially, automatically give more credence to young, new, dynamic personalities than the adults they see every day. I remember being a teen going to the barber and asking for a haircut like Donovan's. Unfortunately, this was the late 70's and no one knew who Donovan was any more. All the other guys in my class wanted to look like John Travolta. This placed me on the high school social chart somewhere between freak and nerd... I was a ferd. I only found comfort in the fact that Donovan's 'Universal Soldier' was clearly more socially significant than 'Greased Lightning'. Spoken like a true ferd.

But people's tendency to emulate heroes they don't actually know doesn't mean we have to feed into this immature mindset. Maybe if the parents and pastors and teachers and grandparents did a better job coming alongside young people, they wouldn't be so distracted by the wind, earthquakes and fire.

In the book of I Jesters 19, in might read like this:

"Now there was a great music festival, with wailing guitars, and performers with hairstyles every bit as cool as their secular counterparts, but the Lord wasn't in the festival... and after the festival, a youth rally, with a hot twenty-something youth pastor whose abs were admired by all the teen girls when they saw him during free swim; and his pretty wife, who all the teenage boys lusted after, but the Lord was not in the youth rally...and after the youth rally, a week of revival meetings featuring a bestselling author who the folks in the little church couldn't believe would come to their small town, but the Lord was not in the revival meetings;

"But after the revival meetings there was the balding, potbellied pastor who worked faithfully and often thanklessly, for his church for decade after decade; there was the school lunch lady who hosted neighborhood girls in her home every weekend to teach them baking and tell them about Jesus, (and even the girls' mothers remember going to the lunch lady's house when they were little girls); there was the chubby teenaged boy who went unnoticed by his peers until someone was being bullied, then he faithfully stood up for what was right without a second thought; there was the aged widow who taught Sunday school week after week, year after year, and always had lollipops for the third graders after the lesson was taught; and it was here that the still, small voice of the Lord can be heard."

Fallacies, Clichés, and Just Plain Stupid Ideas that have Infiltrated the Church World

We all hear them; the clichés, beliefs and myths that are commonly said around the pot luck table or the fellowship hour coffee urn. Sometimes they're said from pulpits, sometimes they're printed on posters. They're in our magazines and music, and we often accept them as truth. Unfortunately, they are frequently NOT truth, and this often hurts our decisions and attitudes in the church world. It is time to set the record straight.

1) "You are now entering the mission field." This sign, often hung over exit doors of churches, promotes the notion that anywhere we go is a mission field. It is meant to inspire Christians to reach out to those who live and work all around them. Unfortunately, this slogan has often caused a much more negative response. If our neighborhood, family or workplace is a mission field, why bother going to, say, North Africa, the Middle East or China to serve there. After all, our coworkers - even if one did muster up the courage to actually reach out to them - won't likely kill us for what we have to say. Biblically, however, 'missions' has always referred to going to unreached people groups; going to those in our surrounding communities may be service, evangelism, or ministry, it is not missionary work.

2) "Most people who accept Jesus become believers under the age of 18." As Mark Twain said, "There are three types of lies: lies, damn lies and statistics." While technically it is true that, in middle class American church culture, most 'conversion experiences' happen to kids under 18, if you factor out kids already growing up in evangelical churches, this is no longer close to the truth. In the 'un-churched' world, most conversions occur among adults in their 20's, 30's, and 40's. In fact, research overwhelmingly shows that the best way to evangelize a family is to reach the fathers, not the kids. Of course, adult men are more intimidating than children, they expect better presentations and have more intelligent arguments to counter the Gospel, so we cling to the misleading statistic above, and spend a disproportionate amount of resources on children's ministry. It's just so much easier that way.

3) "Love the sinner, hate the sin." A) Let's get it straight, this is not a verse of scripture. B) It's degrading. The fact is, we are all sinners. We live our lives on one side or the other of the grace provided by the resurrection, but we're all it this together. C) We're so darn good at hating the sin; one might conclude we actually hate the sinners, too. D) If we truly love the sinner, we won't have to go around telling others that we love the sinner. Did Mother Teresa have to tell people what an incredible lover she was?

4) "God will never give you more than you can handle." This is also not scripture. The Bible does say we won't be tempted beyond what we can handle, which, to me, makes sense. Otherwise, we're all just like Flip Wilson saying, "The devil made me do it." But the fact is we have self-control. This is very different from the above platitude, however. For example, could this cliché have helped my former employee, Patrick, who could no longer afford his medication, spiraled into a dark tunnel of depression, and took his own life? Could it bring any comfort to Patrick's parents? His friends? I think not. Sometimes even the best of believers just can't take it anymore. That's why we need each other to hold up our arms and wipe away our tears.

5) "Christian music, TV, literature, etc." The truth is the word "Christian" was never meant to be an adjective. In fact, it was originally a slur against this new, radical sect of the first century. Roman historian Tacitus wrote, "The vulgar call them Christians." This word is used only three times in all of Scripture, and it is always derogatory. Then, second century believers did to the 'C' word what some urban black youth have done with the 'N' word and gay activists have done with the 'Q' word. They began using it themselves to take the sting out of it. Still, it is a word that should, at best, label who we are, not describe a genre of music, and never, EVER, to describe a political affiliation.

6)   "America is (was, must become) a Christian nation." Certainly, our Constitution refers to the Creator and Scripture.   Certainly, most of the colonies were founded, at least in part, by people of faith: Catholics in Maryland, Puritans in New England, Quakers in Pennsylvania, etc. But the fact is Jesus made it clear that theocracies were to become a thing of the past. While Israel was both the people of God and a nation of God, the new covenant was for all peoples. Thus He told his followers to be like salt and yeast: a small yet vital presence in all nations. A presence, yes, but not a monarchy.

7) "Jesus is coming, are you ready?" I see two errors in this statement. I sincerely believe, that, while the end of history is a clear prophesy throughout Scripture, the details do NOT 'all line up' yet. The strongest support I have for this view is that a full 1/3 of all language groups have no Gospel presence. This 1/3 is, statistically, a small percentage of the world's actual population, but it takes just as much time and effort to reach a small language / people group as it does to reach a large one. Perhaps more. And scripture is clear that ALL nations, tribes and tongues would be represented in the kingdom of God. Furthermore, the fear of Jesus returning is not the way to do evangelism. All mentions of the end of history in Scripture were directed toward the church to tell them to get their act together. Evangelism was always about hope and grace, not fear.

How I Spent the Day the World Ended, and the Years that Followed
(Inspired by "Arab spring")

Once again, events in the Middle East are sending the faithful (or should I say fearful) scrambling for their Bibles and dusting off copies of Hal Lidsey and Tim LaHaye books. I remember, as a young Christian, finding it very confusing when the fall of the Iron Curtain had this same effect on fellow believers then: "Gorbachev will be killed and rise up again in three day; That birthmark on his head is really the mark of the beast; Freedom coming to these Communist countries is all part of Satan's master plan;" on and on it went.

Then came Desert Storm. Sue and I were trying to conceive our first child then, and I remember a sister in Christ saying, "We're on the verge of war, the economy's a mess, the end is near, and here you are trying to start a family." Some encouragement! That particular story ends with us having three daughters, the world not ending yet, and the misguided lady getting divorced.

And who alive at the time can forget the classic book "88 Reasons Why Jesus Will Return in 1988"? A woman we knew at the time said, "I don't believe in date setting, but I'm staying home on the 11th (the day in 1988 when Jesus was to return) just to be sure." 'What's the point of that?' I silently wondered.

We, by comparison, spent that evening juggling in the Windham, Maine Shopping Mall. No trumpets sounded there, either, but if Jesus *had* returned that day, I'd like to think He'd prefer to find us there preaching His Word than home hiding under our beds. Ironically, author Edgar Whisenant wrote a sequel to his book the next year, "89 Reasons Jesus Will Return in 1989". I wish I was joking, but it's true. If this were Old Testament times, I'm not sure there'd be enough stones for all the false prophets.

Of course, the end times were really going to start in conjunction with the Y2K crisis, perhaps the biggest urban legend ever circulated. I kinda believed this one for a while, but we didn't have the money to stockpile food, and had to keep dipping into whatever small cache we had. In October, 1999, "Cornerstone" ran an article exposing the myth for what it was, and we stopped being concerned. Upon the arrival of the new millennium, prison doors didn't spring open, planes didn't plunge from the sky, and no united world government rose up to solve the crisis.

It was in 2008, of course, that US voters elected the anti-Christ for President. This confused me, too, because I'm pretty convinced Emperor Nero fit the biblical description of the 'man of lawlessness' much more precisely than Mr. Obama does. But books about Nero don't sell nearly as many copies as the "Left Behind" series did, and it's hard for TBN newscasters to get people fired up about Nero's abuses since they happened way back in 70 AD. False prophecies sell so much better.

So what do I make of the revolutions in the Middle East? I'm not sure, but it certainly seems God, not Satan, is on the move. He's in charge, and He's not sleeping on the job; nor is He a doddering old fool who is unaware of events here on earth. He's got our backs, and He's got the backs of our brothers and sisters around the world. We need not hide under our beds. He holds the future firmly in His hands, and some day history *will* cease. May He find us faithful, not fearful.

Brown-Eyed Susans, Canada Geese, and International Travel

On Tuesday, our oldest daughter, Jo, is returning from Uganda where she did a ten week internship in an orphanage. Sue, Rose and I, in turn, are flying out to Paraguay on Thursday. We will have two more weeks with Jo once we return before she heads off to college and, between traveling to a friend's wedding and getting her sister Naomi all to herself, our being away is, in her eyes, no problem at all. In my eyes, however, I see one more reason to worry and doubt. "Should we have scheduled our trip so close to her return? Will our oldest two be OK at home without us? Is international travel safe? Are airplanes safe? Did I really hear from God about Paraguay, or am I leading my family based on my own agendas? Am I a good dad?" It's amazing how these thought can come so quickly and strongly.

So this is what I've been wrestling with in recent days. While mulling all this over, it occurred to me that I confuse worrying with caring. I don't know where I get this from, and I guess that doesn't really matter. The fact is I have it wrong. Worrying isn't an indication of how much I care, it's an indication of how little I trust.

Worrying's not a sign of a big heart, it's a sign of tiny faith. Caring is demonstrated by planning, providing, and praying. It's demonstrated by making sound and safe decisions. But worrying does not equal caring. In fact, I've heard it called the anti-meditation. Instead of reflecting on the truth and goodness of God, worry has us thinking about lies and problems that may very well never come to be.

Then, yesterday, Rose and I were doing a show at the Bridgton Health Care Center, our local nursing home. I was ending the program with a flower box production and talking about Jesus' words from the Sermon on the Mount; "And why do you worry about clothes? See how the flowers of the field grow. They do not labor or spin. Yet I tell you that not even Solomon in his entire splendor was dressed like one of these. If that is how God clothes the grass of the field, which is here today and tomorrow is thrown into the fire, will he not much more clothe you — you of little faith?" Without any prior planning, a thought came to me next and was immediately out of my mouth to the audience:

"And why do I worry about flying to South America. Look at the Canadian geese. They don't use planes, but the Father brings them on migrations from one end of the world to the other. Are we not worth more than geese?"

I then reminded the audience that, as they look out their windows and see the brown-eyed Susans growing in the unmown field adjacent to their home, to let those wild flowers be a reminder of God's promise to care for us. And as I see the geese in local fields fattening up for their upcoming flight south, they must also be a reminder to me that He is good, and He is in control. I need not worry.

I Think I'm a Snob

I think I'm a snob. I never thought I was before, and people tell me I'm not, but the Lord has been convicting me this summer that, in fact, I'm a snob. My snobbery has nothing to do with materialism, as my wife and I are on the lower end of middle class, and we still live in a mobile home. It has nothing to do with talents, because, if anything, I'm more likely to see myself as inadequate in all that I do.

I'm a dream snob.

The Lord is showing me that I am critical, though only to myself and other likeminded snobs- never publically, of people who don't have what I consider 'big' dreams. It makes me sad, for example, when kids get married right out of high school or even right after college. I consider it almost a moral failure when people want to live in the same place where they grew up. I silently laugh at people who consider a 100 mile drive to be a long venture. And deep down, I've always felt the movie "It's a Wonderful Life" was really about a poor sap giving up on his dreams and settling for the status quo. Not real inspiring when you look at it that way.

You see, I love to be busy, to see new places, do new things and meet new people. Even though we stay very active in our ministry, including frequent mission trips, I often crave more: More new experiences, more excitement. There's nothing wrong with that, but it's not the only right way to live.

So how did the Lord convict me of this sin of snobbery? It wasn't through a sermon, devotional, or earthquake. It was through a tee-shirt. There's a young woman we know, a recent high school graduate, who plans to get married in a year and live in the same rural town she grew up in. My immediate response is to be both sad and indignant that she has no bigger dreams than that.

Then I saw her in a 'Walk for Life' tee shirt the other day. Like a left hook to the jaw, it hit me. She's walking to benefit the unborn and for single moms right where God has planted her. Her home town needs people like her, and she wants to be there. How can that be a bad thing? Maybe serving God while living within the status quo is just as important as serving God while living out big dreams.

Don't get me wrong. I still crave our next mission trip, our next visit to prison, and I sure hope our girls really are called to their current big dreams of missions work. But I can no longer believe that people who want to quietly serve God and others while never straying too far from home, or doing anything more unconventional than a walk-a-thon, are immature, or wrong, or missing out on anything.

I must admit that, for people who find their call is to serve joyfully and faithfully within the status quo, it really is a wonderful life.

Section 5:

FINISHING WITH FAVORITES

I've especially enjoyed writing and rereading these blogs

Harder to Believe than Not To

The other day I learned of a Christian school Bible curriculum that said something to the effect of this: "It's just as easy to believe as to not believe, so why not believe." Putting aside the ridiculous superficiality of this argument, it appalls me that this is being taught by Christian educators. Quite frankly, anyone who's truly tried to follow Christ for more than a few minutes must see the stupidity of this statement.

Tell John the Baptist, as the sword is about to sever his head from his body, it's just as easy to believe as not to. Tell Stephen, as the crowd is smashing his body with rocks until he dies, that it's just as easy to believe as not to. Tell Polycarp, as the flames are scorching his body; Tell Dietrich Bonhoeffer as he's walked to the gallows of the Nazi concentration camp, tell Martin Luther King Jr. as the dogs are turned loose on his nonviolent marchers; Tell Mother Teresa who gave up a life of affluence to bathe lepers on the streets of Calcutta; Tell Rachel Scott and Cassie Burnell, who were murdered at Columbine High School for their strong beliefs in Jesus; Tell faithful teens and single adults who are trying to save their virginity to be a sacred gift to their future spouses in a culture that mocks them; Tell it to Christians in North Korea, Iran and Syria. If we were able to, they would wonder where we got such a laughable notion and agree instead with writer Flannery O'Connor: "It's harder to believe than not to."

Of course, even a little experience with the Scriptures confirms O'Connor's words. We're told to lay down our lives, carry our crosses, go the extra mile, turn the other cheek, take the narrow way, and that we're not our own. We're told to love our enemies, pray for those who persecute us, always forgive, welcome the outcast and rejoice when we're persecuted. We're told to not only worship, but imitate an itinerant Rabbi whose life was cut brutally short due to trumped up charges, the betrayal of a friend and political maneuvering.

I agree that mentally assenting to a theology- often the extent of what's expected in the suburban Gospel- is just as easy as unbelief, but assenting to theological ideas is not faith. The biblical concept of belief is better described as discipleship... believing to the point of giving up everything that might get in the way and following with our whole lives. There's nothing easy about that, but when we encounter the flood of grace Christ wants to pour over us, it is so worth it.

Pope Francis, Rush Limbaugh and Jesus Christ: One of These Things is not Like the Other

Apparently this week, FOX "News" reporter Rush Limbaugh attacked Pope Francis's statement that "Unfettered capitalism" was "tyranny" and trickledown economics did not work. Not surprisingly, Rush's love of money (hmmm... where have I heard that phrase before?) didn't allow him to stay silent. He declared Pope Francis to be a Marxist who "doesn't know what he's talking about."

Before going any further, I must say that I do not accept the papacy as my spiritual authority. No one man should have that much influence on what millions of people think about God. Only *God* should have that much influence on what people think about God, through Scripture, mediation and the teaching and counsel of a wide variety of learned men and women ("One plants, another waters, but the Lord provides the harvest," Paul said.) Both my wife and I were raised Catholic, and we have both since left the Catholic Church. On the other hand, some of the most influential people in my Christian growth have been members of the Roman Catholic church, including my mom, my college roommate, and our best friends for the past 25 years. I am neither a Pope bashing fundy nor a 'what he says goes' follower of the pontiff. So, when Rush made these statements, I didn't look into it with the notion that the Pope is always right or that Limbaugh, the pope of the right, was necessarily wrong.

While the success of trickledown economics in the US is still an issue of debate - I remember the 1980's being a fairly prosperous time - I am convinced it is no solution to third world poverty, where much of the destitution has more to do with intentional tribal and religious oppression than individuals' work ethic. Nothing ever trickles down, it seems, to the Tarahumaran of Mexico, the rural Quichuan of the Andes or the Enxet of Paraguay's Chaco region. And this economy of racism would be all too familiar to the Argentinian Pope. Rush, on the other hand, has likely not ventured into the third world very much. Of course there was that infamous trip to the Dominican Republic where he was detained at the Santo Domingo airport for possession of a prescription of Viagra that was not his own, but my guess is he was not there to visit the dump community or the street kids living in the barrios. Call it a hunch.

On the other hand, Pope Francis' approach seems to be a combination of pie-in-the-sky optimism and vague platitudes. When, for example, millions of Hindus in India believe the poor are *supposed to be poor* based on centuries of religious tradition, how possibly will things change for them? (Yes, the caste system is now 'illegal' in India, but ask any recent immigrant if things have changed there.)

In Paraguay learned that as recently as the 1970's, they had a president who banned iodized salt because iodine aids in brain development (up to 15 IQ points, to be precise.)   It was El Presidente's way of intentionally keeping the tribal people poorly educated, thus easy to control which means, of course, poor. For the billions of people worldwide who live in *these* realities no amount of talk about wealth redistribution is going to help, because it won't ever happen. Perhaps the Pope himself could help, though, by redistributing some of his church's $422,098,000,000 annual income. I will never forget site seeing in Quito, Ecuador. We happened upon a Catholic church that charged admission to see its ornate gold statues. Meanwhile, an old, weathered Quechan woman begged for pennies outdoors on the church's steps. Ready to put your money where your mouth is and live up to the name of St. Francis, your holiness? Then set an example to the rest of the world's wealthy and redistribute some of that.

Perhaps the Catholic Pope and the FOX 'News' dope have more in common than it first appears.   Both are saying a lot but not doing much. Both are concerned about prosperity. They just disagree on how to get there. But Jesus turns the whole discussion of economics on its head (as he so often did with a variety of other topics as well) when he told a rich young ruler, "Sell all your possessions, give everything to the poor, and follow me." (Mark 10:21.) Another time he said, "Do not store up treasures on earth where moths and rust can destroy them" (Matthew 6:19.) Similarly, John wrote, "Do not love the world or the things of this world," while Paul told us "The love of money is the root of all evil."

Perhaps the wrong question is being asked. Perhaps it's not so much who should be rich or how people can prosper more, but, "What is life really about in the first place?"

Of Water Boards and Crosses

I've often wondered about the Republican Party's thinking leading into the election of 2008. It seems that, after two terms under George W., who was a solid C student in college, they felt a need to find someone with a worse GPA to be his predecessor. Enter John McCain, third from last in his class at West Point. But of course he couldn't have a running mate smarter than himself, so it seems they searched far and wide until they found someone even dimmer: Sarah Palin. Okay, I'll admit McCain is both brighter than his GPA would indicate and a legitimate war hero and I respect him for that. Furthermore, I have to accept that Palin, in spite of being misguided about almost everything, professes to be a fellow believer (as does McCain when he needs the evangelical vote) so I must love her as a sister.

It's just so darn hard.

Last week, at a national NRA rally before tens of thousands of members, Palin told the crowd of gun owners that water boarding is how she would 'baptize terrorists'.

Never mind that torture has been proven to be an ineffective way of getting information from prisoners.

Never mind that the NRA tries to disguise itself as an organization for sportsmen.

Never mind Mrs. Palin claims to build her life on the One who said "Love your enemy" and "turn the other cheek".

Never mind that this type of rhetoric makes both America and Christians look bad.

The NRA crowd roared with approval.

Read about it here: http://www.huffingtonpost.com/rabbi-menachem-creditor/sarah-palin-nra_b_5235427.html

Worst, of course, is that she used the biblical rite of baptism not only lightly but *blasphemously*. Baptism is to show one's identification with the burial and resurrection of the Messiah, and the first act of obedience commanded of Christians. To liken it to torture is horrendous, and I hope she publically repents of her words. I find myself wanting to scream, "Not all Christians are like that."

The same day I read about this NRA rally, I read an article about Muslim extremists in Syria who have started publicly crucifying those who speak out against them.

Read about it here:
http://www.cnn.com/2014/05/01/world/meast/syria-bodies-crucifixions/index.html

This is being carried out by ISIS, a fringe group considered too radical even for al Qaida. No doubt there are many Muslims around the world screaming, "Not all Muslims are like that." While the religious significance of a crucifixion is obvious, the article claims it was not necessarily for religious symbolism that they chose crucifixion for their victims, but rather for political reasons. Of course, in the Middle East, religion and politics are inseparable.

Seeing the photos of young men suffering in agony as blood ran down their pierced wrists and little children looking on, I thought again about Sarah Palin's desire to baptize these people with pain. I've gotta say, a part of me felt the adrenaline rush that comes from vengeful fantasies as I imagined the crucifiers suffering brutally from torture. But then I was reminded of the most famous crucifixion in history: A sacrifice for the sins of all and any who might believe. Why couldn't an Islamic extremist become a follower of Jesus? Members of street gangs have; Mafia members have; Heck, Son of Sam is a pastor in his maximum security prison. Jesus, it seems, would rather see these thugs baptized into the church, not into torment.

The real lesson for Mrs. Palin, and all of us, is that religion, particularly Christianity, but certainly all three of the Abrahamic faiths, is all about not giving in to our base desires for revenge (or greed, or ego, or etc. etc.) and take the high road when our natural instinct is not to.

It's just so darn hard.

An Open Letter to Tom Petty

Dear Tom,

It was with sincere pleasure that I heard about your upcoming release of an all new album entitled "Hypnotic Eye". I have always enjoyed your music. I was especially interested in reading your interview in Billboard regarding this release. The article seemed to focus almost entirely on your song "Playing Dumb", which is your response to the child molestation issue within the Catholic Church. Thank you for keeping this all important issue in the public eye. I especially respect your statement, "If I was in a club, and I found out that there had been generations of people abusing children, and then that club was covering that up, I would quit the club."

However, Tom, I want to caution you about painting with too wide of a brush. While I'll admit I left the Catholic Church years ago over some theological issues, we both need to admit there are many sincere, admirable Catholic people. From Francis of Assisi to Father Flanagan to Mother Teresa, there have always been those who truly serve the biblical Jesus within Catholicism.

And for every household name, there's hundreds of thousands of others humbly living their lives of sincere faith. Let me tell you about Sister Maximillian. She was once a self-professed wild child who had an encounter with Jesus as a teen. She is serving this same Jesus year in and year out at a children's home in New Hampshire. She and several other nuns work with the children the foster care system has let down, as she herself puts it. I know this lady, she's real. She's a hero to our daughters. Don't insult her with your generalizations about the 1.2 billion people who profess Catholicism. Would you generalize about other groups - blacks, Arabs, rock musicians - based on the behavior of some? I doubt it, and Catholics deserve the same treatment.

Later in the interview you say, "Religion seems to me to be at the base of all wars." As an educator, Tom, I have to say you are really off base on this. Greed and pride are the basis for most wars in history. None of the wars ever fought by the United States were religious in nature.

None.

And even wars that seem to be religious in nature rarely are. In the 1970's and 80's there was the fighting between Protestant and Catholic in Northern Ireland. The real issue, though, was whether or not Ireland should be loyal to the British crown or to seek independence. It was never a theological issue, and, in fact, there have always been Protestants on the 'Catholic' side of the issue and vice versa.

Of course, there have been some religious wars, most notably the Crusades. In such situations, I agree with you when you say, "I've nothing against defending yourself, but I don't think, spiritually speaking, that there's any conception of God that should be telling you to be violent." I would take it one step further, actually, and say that even worse is when, in a secular war, nations claim that God is on their side alone. Sounds kinda like of a Dylan song, doesn't it?

You continue by saying, "It seems to me that no one's got Christ more wrong than the Christians." This is not a new sentiment, even among song writers. From Joe Hill's "Pie in the Sky" written in 1911 to Crosby, Stills and Nash's "Cathedral" to the more recent "Jesus, Jesus" by Noah Gunderson, hypocrisy in the church has been a familiar theme of popular music.

When I see false prophets like Harold Camping and Pat Robertson, and prosperity gospel con men like Joel Osteen and Benny Hinn, I am tempted to agree with you.

But again, we must resist the temptation to paint with a broad brush. Did Martin Luther King get Christ wrong as he marched for justice in Selma, Alabama? Did William Wilberforce get Christ wrong as he fought slavery in England's parliament for 17 years?

Did William Booth get Christ wrong when he took on poverty and child labor during Britain's industrial revolution and started the Salvation Army? Did Harriet Beecher Stowe get Christ wrong when she and her pastor-husband took on slavery and changed history with their preaching and her novel "Uncle Tom's Cabin"? Did David Wilkerson get Christ wrong when he gave up everything to start an outreach to gang members and addicts in the inner city; a work that has spread worldwide over the last half century? I think not. Having lived your life in the limelight, you must realize that the media likes sensationalistic stories, so it is the extremists among Christians who get the press coverage. Visit a local church and get to know the real people there professing faith in Jesus. I bet your opinion will change.

Furthermore, hypocrisy in the church should come as no surprise to anyone. Jesus said there would be "weeds sown among the wheat", false disciples living among the sincere believers. Your frustration with 'Christians who don't get Christ' only proves Jesus' words on this topic to be true. I'm not surprised when I see hypocrisy in the church. But I'm also not surprised when I see sincere, loving believers pouring their lives out for God and others.

Finally, your statement seems to imply that you do "get Christ". I hope this is true because He is nothing short of amazing!

So, if you consider yourself someone who 'gets Christ', let me ask you how you're doing with Him? How are doing with loving your enemy? Being a peace maker? Giving all you have to follow him? Please understand, I am not asking this facetiously. It is a "narrow road", and we need accountability. I will pray for you as you seek to 'get him' more and more, and I would ask you pray for me as well.

Respectfully,

Richard A Hagerstrom

PS Thank you for the music. High school really would not have been the same without it.

When the Perfect 10 Falls in Love With a Mental Case

I have been a fan of Bob Newhart for decades. Whether it's his standup comedy, his sketches - who can forget Sir Walter Raleigh on the telephone with King George explaining how tobacco will be the next cash crop of the southern colonies - or his oddball sitcoms, he has always made me laugh. His TV shows have left me wondering one thing, though. Do they really expect us to believe that a short, balding stutterer like Newhart could end up with wives such as Suzanne Pleshette and Mary Frann? I suppose it's possible, but it gets me thinking about beauty and the beast marriages. As rare as they are, rarer still is when the beauty is the groom, not the bride. When does the football hero ever end up with the self-loathing wall flower?

The angry Goth chick?

The unstable drama queen who practically lives in the guidance counselor's office?

Unlikely.

But...

If the church - not the church as institution, not a denomination, but the church defined as the followers of Jesus, the universal body of believers - is the bride of Christ, then maybe there's hope for the wallflower, Goth chick or mental case in all of us.

Jesus is passionately in love with those who bear his name. The perfect 10 has fallen for a mental case. The Lion of Judah is head over heels for a dung slinging baboon. The King of Kings has given His heart to a peasant wench. "Let us be glad and rejoice, and give honor to him: for the marriage of the Lamb is come, and his wife hath made herself ready," says the book of Revelation. Several times in the epistles, Paul, too, compares the church to the bride of Jesus. The church, in all our dysfunction, pride and immaturity, is, nonetheless, the object of Christ's affection.

Millennials, I have read, are embracing Christ while rejecting church at an ever increasing rate, and I understand very well why they might want to do this. As Gandhi said, "I like your Christ; I do not like your Christians. Your Christians are so unlike your Christ." I could echo Gandhi's sentiments with story after story of disappointments I've had at the hands of Christians.

But, if Christians are the bride of Christ, to reject the church is to reject the object of Jesus' ultimate delight. Yes, the church. The church that is much too concerned with political power, and not concerned enough with poverty and prayer. The church that exploits Christ as a means to acquiring the American dream. The church that rationalizes, resents, rages and rebels. *That church* is the bride of the Messiah, and He adores her unapologetically, unconditionally and unabashedly.

There's an old guy in our town named Frank. Years ago, his wife of 50 plus years developed severe dementia, but old Frank never stopped adoring her. When she had no idea who he was, he still adored her. When he had to hire someone to dress and bathe her, he still adored her. When she treated him as a stranger, or, worse, a threat, he still adored her. He had her in a nursing home for a while, but couldn't bare it. He brought her home. Old Frank is a farmer in rural Maine, so he doesn't articulate how much he cherishes Norma, but when he holds her hand, walks her into church, kisses her cheek, he speaks of love more beautifully than all the words Shakespeare has ever written. Frank and Norma remind me of Jesus' love for his church. One sided, illogical, unending.

Jesus likened the church to a field growing both wheat (true followers) and weeds (people who are involved with the Christian religion but without any sincere faith). He ends the parable by saying it wasn't the job of the wheat to try to rid the field of the weeds. I'm not proud of it, but I'd LOVE that job. I'd love to go from church to church and decide who was worthy and who was not. But then I think of all those who, if given the same opportunity, would want to weed ME out. I know there would be plenty. But Jesus said, in essence, "Don't you dare wax that unibrow or straighten those crooked teeth. Those could very well be the parts of my bride that I love the most."

You see, the marriage feast of the lamb, unlike virtually all modern day weddings, isn't about the bride, it's about the groom.

A groom who, as Brennan Manning put it in his classic devotional "The Ragamuffin Gospel", expects us to fail even more than we expect ourselves to. A groom who tells his bride, as song writer Charlie Peacock wrote, "Cheer up church, you're worse off than you think." A groom who, like Saint Paul said, "Might sanctify her, having cleansed her by the washing of water with the word, that He might present to Himself the church in all her glory, having no spot or wrinkle or any such thing; but that she would be holy and blameless."

Make no mistake, the perfect love of Jesus for his church isn't blind to the church's 'spots and wrinkles'. He does better than turn a blind eye. His is a love that delivers the beast from the very curse that stole its beauty to begin with.

Why Don't You Look into Jesus

In 1973, Larry Norman recorded arguably the greatest, most influential Contemporary Christian music album ever recorded. "Only Visiting This Planet" changed Gospel music forever, and, 39 years later is still very listenable and even still a bit edgy. His "Why Don't You Look Into Jesus?" is one of the best cuts on this landmark album, and is the music I use with my club juggling routine

I was thinking about Norman's question today. It was an excellent question in 1973, when many in the baby boom generation were exploring Zen, TM, Satanism (authentic and the lunatic fringe), and a wealth of other philosophies and religions. It is an equally good question today when so many have little to no religious training; isn't it worth at least looking into the claims of Jesus to see what they are and if they have any significance today.

Then one very good reason someone might hesitate to 'look into Jesus' came to mind. I've heard this said innumerable different ways, but basically it can be stated like this: "I tried Jesus, and it (He) didn't work." To this I reply, "What Jesus did you try?"

If one looks into the Jesus of con men like Benny Hinn, it's no wonder they end up bitter. If one looks into the Jesus of Sarah Palin – a Jesus of nationalistic superiority – it is no wonder they end up lukewarm in heart.

If one looks into the Jesus of Joel Osteen and the health & wealth Gospel, it's no wonder they end up disappointed. If one looks into the wishy-washy Jesus of Rob Bell, it's no wonder they decide Jesus just isn't important.

But what about the real Jesus; Jesus according to Jesus? What about the Jesus who never promised health or wealth, but rather offered a life of trials and simplicity, but an abundant life nonetheless? What about the Jesus who confronted con men, both religious (the Pharisees) and secular (Zacchaeus)? What about the Jesus who went out of his way to confront racial bigotry at every opportunity; after all, what other Rabbi would have ever told a story in which the hero was a Samaritan? What about the Jesus who promised us nothing in this life except grace for our failures and direction in life's trials, but went on to say those would be sufficient for us? What about the Jesus who said, "I am the Way the Truth and the Life; no man comes to the Father except through me."

So, like Larry Norman asked 39 years ago, I ask you, "Why don't you look into Jesus?"

Made in the USA
Middletown, DE
21 February 2016